Make Me a Blessing

YOUR ORDINARY LIFE CAN HAVE ETERNAL IMPACT

Cassia Elder

ISBN 978-0-578-52393-4
Library of Congress Control Number: 2019906542

Unless otherwise noted, all Scripture is taken from: The Holy Bible, New International Version®, NIV®. Copyright © 1973, 1978, 1984, 2011 by Biblica, Inc.® Used by permission. All rights reserved worldwide.

Scripture marked (ESV): The Holy Bible, English Standard Version. Copyright © 2001 by Crossway Bibles, a publishing ministry of Good News Publishers. Text Edition: 2016. All rights reserved.

Scripture marked (MSG): *THE MESSAGE*. Copyright © by Eugene H. Peterson,1993, 1994, 1995, 1996, 2000, 2001, 2002. Used by permission of NavPress Publishing Group.

Scripture marked (NLT): The Holy Bible, New Living Translation. Copyright © 1996, 2004, 2015 by Tyndale House Foundation. Used by permission of Tyndale House Publishers, Inc., Carol Stream, Illinois 60188. All rights reserved.

Scripture marked (NLV): New Life Version. Copyright © 1969 and 2003. Used by permission of Barbour Publishing, Inc., Uhrichsville, Ohio 44683. All rights reserved.

Scripture marked (NASB): New American Standard Bible®. Copyright © 1960,1962,1963,1968,1971,1972,1973,1975,1977,1995 by The Lockman Foundation. Used by permission.

Scripture marked (NKJV): New King James Version®. Copyright © 1982 by Thomas Nelson. Used by permission. All rights reserved.

Scripture marked (NET): The NET Bible®, New English Translation. Copyright © 1996 by Biblical Studies Press, L.L.C. NET Bible® is a registered trademark. The NET Bible® logo, service mark copyright © 1997 by Biblical Studies Press, L.L.C. All rights reserved.

Cover Design by Cori Horvath
Author Photo by B+N Photography

Cover Photograph is a detail from *Mosaic with Imago Clipeata of Bacchus*: Roman, from Tunisia, Floor Mosaic, about 140 – 160 A.D., polychrome marble and glass tesserae set in grouting, width 9 ft. 10 3/8 in., length 9 ft. 9 1/2 in., Toledo Museum of Art, Purchased with funds from the Libbey Endowment, Gift of Edward Drummond Libbey, 1990.73

To Chris and Asa.
You are my two most favorite blessings.

I make every effort to connect with you as transparently as possible. Our lives are purposefully and inseparably intertwined with the lives of others. So, I am also intentional to protect the hearts and the privacy of those people whose stories intersect with mine. The personal stories in this book are completely true. In most instances, friends and family have graciously granted me permission to share with you their stories and their part in my story. In some other places, I have changed names and inconsequential details, like locations or events, for the privacy of others while maintaining the integrity of the situation.

Contents

INTRODUCTION

Uniquely Unqualified

Welcome, friend! I write to you from the weathered back porch of our rustic log cabin on a nearly-off-grid microfarm. I wish you were sitting next to me on my grandma's hand-me-down porch swing as I share my story. I live a simple, ordinary life. I am not a Bible scholar. I do not have a seminary degree or any other degree for that matter. I do not hold an important position or an impressive title. I am uniquely unqualified to bring to you the message of *Make Me a Blessing*.

Many of us wonder if our day-to-day lives matter at all. Can we really make a difference? I mean, we are "Just a mom. Just a receptionist. Just a factory worker." Over the past several years, I have been learning and living out the message of *Make Me a Blessing*. God has been teaching me how ordinary people can have eternal impact while living our everyday lives. Despite my unqualification, I have seen my own small contributions become blessing in the lives of others. In fact, being unqualified is perhaps the very thing that qualifies me most to demonstrate why a person does not need to be qualified in the eyes of the world in order to be used by God. "The LORD does not look at the things people look at. People look at the outward appearance, but the LORD looks at the heart," 1 Samuel 16:7b. God doesn't look at your resumé or ask for credentials. Honestly, the only prerequisite He desires is a heart willing to be used by Him.

My friend Kristen sent the photo that hung above my desk, "God doesn't call the qualified. He qualifies the called." That. Is. Truth. Laced throughout Scripture are stories of ordinary, beyond unlikely characters who God used to impact eternity.

"When they saw the courage of Peter and John and realized that they were unschooled, *ordinary* men, they were astonished and they took note that these men had been with Jesus," Acts 4:13 (*emphasis mine*). Oh, dear sister, isn't that the point? When people see what God accomplishes with our ordinary lives, they will know it is not because of our qualification, but because of our relationship with Jesus. God uses ordinary people to make an extraordinary difference. That way, He gets all the glory.

Our culture has instilled in us a preoccupation, dare I say an obsession, with finding our one true purpose. We get caught up in the search for the big picture of our lives. We are driven to wrap up who we are in a single, meaningful word. Teacher. Pastor. Missionary. Author. When we surrender to being used by God, He may direct us to further education; He may elevate us to position; He may bestow on us a title; He may grace us with credentials. But we cannot look to those things to qualify us. We can't wait for something big to happen before we begin to bless. As a young boy, David was anointed by Samuel to be king. But he didn't wait until he was older, stronger, or more influential to make a difference. David was uniquely unqualified in stature, position, and experience when he boldly stood "in the name of the LORD

Almighty, the God of the armies of Israel"[1] and slayed that giant.

Big picture, forward thinking in exclusion can result in not seeing the trees for the forest. We need to zoom in. Our sovereign God brought each one of us right to where we are for such a time as this. Like me, you are uniquely unqualified to meet the needs in your own circle of influence. Your purpose is not tied up in your 5-year plan. Your time is now. "Why, you do not even know what will happen tomorrow. What is your life? You are a mist that appears for a little while and then vanishes," James 4:14.

You have a Right. Now. Purpose.

Please don't misunderstand, purpose is powerful. We don't have to search to find our one true purpose. You. Me. Every human. All of creation. We all have a common, singular, one-and-only purpose: to bring glory to God. We do that in two distinct ways: through our personal relationship with Him and through our relationships with others. *Make Me a Blessing* is all about the practical ways we bring God glory by blessing others. Each one of us is destined to live it out in a unique way.

We cannot be summed up in one word. Our existence is not about one macro, whole-life mission. We must tune in to our micro, today mission. Hear the whisper of that famous Robin Williams pep talk, "Carpe diem. Seize the day."[2] On an even finer level, each encounter, each interaction is an opportunity to bless. Every life is a collection of a million distinct moments. Eventually, we will understand how our Father, who sees the beginning from the end, pieces it all together. Let's not miss out on the seemingly small opportunities right in front of us because we are distracted by searching for something bigger.

"But God chose the foolish things of the world to shame the wise; God chose the weak things of the world to shame the strong," 1 Corinthians 1:27.

Embrace the Scripture paradox:

> The least is greatest. (Luke 9:48)
> The humble is exalted. (Matthew 23:12)
> The weak is strong. (2 Corinthians 12:10)
> The last is first. (Matthew 20:16)

It only makes sense—the small might actually be big.

Don't wait. You have a Right Now Purpose, in this moment, to be made a blessing.

CHAPTER 1

The Heart of Blessing

As a busy mom, the only thing more infrequent than time alone with my husband was time all alone. Real time alone. Not sneaking away to the bathroom for a sliver of solitude when nanoseconds later banging at the door is accompanied by the most obvious of questions. Honestly! What do they think I'm doing in here? By alone time, I mean a house silent. Not the kind of quiet that shouts back, "I did turn the TV down!"

Please don't misunderstand me. I have an intense adoration for the people God gave me. I also have an occasional soul-deep need for them to go away and leave me alone. Those solitary moments were so few and so far between. Did lightning strike twice? No. An even less likely occurrence. I had the house completely to myself! How does one maximize the most precious of commodities? Take a nap? Clean the house? Watch that chick-flick I've had DVRed for 18 months but never got the chance to watch because I am a boy mom, outnumbered, who always gets stuck watching superhero movies?

When I choose wisely, my alone time becomes my God time. Pray. Read. Study. Worship. Listen. I call these rare moments "Date Night with Jesus." One such unusual night, I flipped on the TV to catch a Bible teacher. Scripture—a promise God spoke to Abraham—scrawled across my screen and with the almost audible sizzle of a branding iron, was emblazoned on my heart.

"I will bless you…. so that you will be a blessing," part of Genesis 12:2 (ESV).

A memory stuffed away. A seed long ago planted, that lay dormant in my soul for 23 years, was at that moment being watered. A song. *Make Me a Blessing* came flooding back, the words flowed from my lips as though I had never stopped singing them.

On that night, God birthed within me a purpose. A calling. Something bigger than myself. A word, not for me alone, but for every blood-bought child of God. We have each been so abundantly blessed that the very purpose of our redeemed lives—to bring glory to God—must be lived out by being made a blessing. We don't start out being a blessing. But Galatians 3:29 says, "If you belong to Christ, then you are Abraham's seed, and heirs according to the promise." So, the promise to us, the seed of Abraham, is just as good as it was the day Jehovah spoke it to Abraham himself. "You will be a blessing."

Having this fresh word burning in my spirit, I had a little pep in my step. I started out right away the next day, intent on being made a blessing. I was not quite sure how to get started, but the mission was clear—to bless other people. When we are awakened to our call to bless, we probably won't immediately be whisked away on an assignment we perceive as doing something big for God. Jet off to the mission field; launch a Billy Graham style crusade. But Zechariah 4:10 tells us not to despise the small beginnings. God will use even the seemingly small and mundane for His glory. In fact, we are promised in God's Word that when we prove to be faithful in the small things, we will be trusted with the larger things

(Luke 16:10). So, the first day, I held doors; I made eye contact and smiled; I gave out my fair share of compliments. Emboldened, by day's end, I knew I was on the right track. This was a good start, but there had to be more to being made a blessing. This message could not be minimized to a good deed for the day. Like a precious gem hiding far beneath the surface, we have to do some excavating to uncover the multifaceted meaning at the heart of blessing. Grab a shovel, friend! We are going to dig in deep together and take a practical approach to discover what blessing truly looks like.

The Top 5 Most Influential People of All Time

1. Jesus Christ- Carpenter, Prophet, Preacher
2. Isaac Newton- Mathematician, Physicist, Chemist
3. Albert Einstein- Mathematician, Physicist, Scientist
4. Leonardo da Vinci- Military Engineer, Musician, Scientist
5. Mary Cribbs- Teacher, Influencer, Inspirer

A Google search uncovers 100s of lists like the one above with just as many variations. This list found at ranker.com[1] had three things in common with all the others I checked out. First, Jesus was at the top of every list. Second, all lists failed to acknowledge Jesus as God or the Son of God. Third, Mary Cribbs did not make any of the lists. Not *Top 5*. Not *Top 100*. Not any other number as far as a list may extend. Not on your list either? I'm not surprised. I added that name. Mary Cribbs was my fifth-grade teacher.

Though she does not top any internet list of influential people, she had a lasting influence in my life and the lives of countless others. If you were to ask anyone who attended Lakota East Elementary School during her time there, I am sure Mrs. Cribbs had their vote for the best teacher EVER, in the entire history of the school, perhaps in the entire history of the world. I cannot possibly articulate what made her so special. If I tried, you would likely think, "I guess you had to be there." My heart aches knowing my words are inadequate to endear her to you. However, the fact that my favorite teacher is, to most, unknown, should give us all hope. Few of us will be truly famous in our own time, let alone in ages to come. We may even wonder if what we're doing really matters at all. We are about to discover together how ordinary people can have eternal impact while living out our everyday lives. If we bless those around us and they are compelled to do the same, our influence will be limitless.

I spent most of the fourth grade and the whole of the summer afterward dreaming of the first day of the next school year when I would finally be *her* student. Rainbow Trapper Keeper? Check! No. 2 pencils? Check! New white canvas tennis shoes? Check! This was it! The day had finally arrived! My turn in Mrs. Cribbs' fifth grade! A warm breeze swept through the third story classroom windows, bringing with it the squeals and smells from the hog farm next door. We enjoyed the fresh country air while we could. It would be only a few weeks now until the windows would be shut back tight to keep corn dust and the rumble of a combine from filling the room.

I had long ago noticed Mrs. Cribbs' brilliant smile, rosy cheeks set off on perfect porcelain skin. Now face-to-face, second seat in the far-left row, the first day of school, she was so beautiful, her face literally seemed to glow! As the year went on, I came to find out the secret of her luminescence. It's the truth mentioned in Psalm 34:5a, "Those who look to him are radiant." When a person's heart is filled with the joy of the Lord, it can't help but show up on their face. You cannot fake that glow, not with the most expensive moisturizer or the most expertly applied makeup. The light of Mrs. Cribbs' countenance was Jesus shining through her. This was also what made her the best teacher ever. She loved Jesus, and His love spilled out of her onto every person in her path. Mrs. Cribbs did not lead me to Jesus, but she inspired me to follow

Him. She modeled the love of God and in turn the love of others. Not always overtly with her words. She lived a life unashamed of the gospel and set the ultimate example of speaking the truth in love. One has little need for compelling words, who tells it all in the life they live.

She knew that I knew Jesus, too. So, Mrs. Cribbs would often give a nudge when my behavior did not reflect Christ living in me. Like the time I called Daniel a dummy. No need for words. Downturned lips and gently furrowed brow spoke volumes. Beyond words.

Mrs. Cribbs talked to us on our level and treated us with the respect of young people; not down to us like mere children, as we had been accustomed. In fact, in our notes back and forth, my teacher called me "friend." That small gesture still leaves a little imprint on my heart. I'm not sure if I ever told her how much that meant to me. I'm not sure I really understood it before now.

In typical fifth grader fashion, I penned inquisitive notes to my teacher.

>"What's your favorite color?"
>"Which flavor of ice cream do you like best?"
>"What is your favorite candy?"

She would graciously respond to my inquiries. Her answers have long ago faded from my memory, except for one.

>"What is your favorite song?"
>She wrote back. "An old hymn, *Make Me a Blessing*."

Rushing from the school bus to the foot of my dad's recliner, I pleaded with him to retrieve the yellow-paged hymnal from higher than my reach on the bookshelf. I plopped to the royal blue carpet, flipping through musty pages, half expecting a moth to flutter out. My eyes grew to saucers as they landed on the page. *Make Me a Blessing* in bold type above rows of staffs. My finger followed clumsily along the notes as I pretended to read the music. The vocabulary was sophisticated and the message tender, as if the composer held a mirror to Mrs. Cribbs' heart. A biography in the form of a ballad. Unfamiliar stirring broke ground in my soul.

We shuffled single file to the basement music room the next Thursday afternoon. I squirmed in my seat, arm straight in the air, hand flapping like the grand ol' flag, for what seemed like ages before the music teacher finally called on me. To my delight, he agreed to keep it a secret and spend a bit of class time each week teaching the fifth graders to sing, *Make Me a Blessing*. Its words, as memorized, implanted in my heart.

Field trips always seemed to occur around the same time spring fever hit. A swaying bus full of rowdy kids returned from the planetarium on that blustery afternoon. The clatter of songs and hand clapping games suddenly hushed. Whispers traveled back and forth, as inconspicuously as 11-year-olds do. Children surrounded our beloved teacher. A lump in my throat was overcome for counting "1, 2, 3!" The Lakota East Elementary Fifth Grade class of 1988 burst into Mrs. Cribbs' favorite song, *Make Me a Blessing*. Like sunshine during the rain, she smiled through tears streaming. Our eyes met with a wink from my teacher, my friend.

Brushing the dust off these old memories, I now sense a wink from my Father, my Friend. The start of my journey, the first time I can remember being made a blessing, was in the singing of the song *Make Me a Blessing*.

Count Your Blessings

The term "blessed" gets tossed around flippantly these days. Overuse and misuse of the word have rendered it nearly meaningless. It has been dwindled down to infer being merely fortunate, lucky. #FeelingBlessed! So what does blessing really look like? What does it mean to be blessed? What are the practical ways for us to be a blessing in our everyday lives? We can redeem the word blessed, return to the original definition, by looking at it in light of God's Word.

James 1:17 tells us, "Every good and perfect gift is from above, coming down from the Father of the heavenly lights, who does not change like shifting shadows." Blessing is not measured by adding up possessions or viewing account balances. It's not a contest where the one with the most toys wins. A person with more material goods is not more blessed than someone with less. Blessing is every good thing in our lives—our families and friends, our health, our time, our talents, our treasure.

Let's take a moment to unpack our key verse in its entirety. (To simplify going forward, we may refer to Genesis 12:2 as our key verse.) "And I will make of you a great nation, and I will bless you and make your name great, so that you will be a blessing," Genesis 12:2 (ESV). The first three phrases of the key verse are what God does. He says, "I will. I will." Whether it's influence— "I will make of you a great nation," or notoriety— "and make your name great," or any other blessing that can be summed up in "I will bless you," it is clear where every gift originates. Blessing comes from one unmistakable Source. Being blessed is no less than endowment by Almighty God with an unmerited gift.

"The earth is the LORD's, and everything in it, the world, and all who live in it;" Psalm 24:1. In the bubble of excess that has become our culture, we can actually start to believe the lie that we've worked hard for everything we have, so we don't owe any of the credit to God. But anything in our possession is not truly ours at all. All that we are and all that we have is a gift from God, and it also belongs to God.

Please know this is a difficult concept to wrap our minds around, but still more difficult to live. That is why you and I are going to link arm in arm right here and try to grow in this together. My son and I discussed this truth recently. He was disproportionately upset about damage that occurred to my car while I was driving. "Stupid pothole!" I told him it's God's car anyway. He will take care of us and the car. "But God gave us the car. Isn't it ours to do with it what we want?" That's how my adult mind thinks too. It may be easier to acknowledge the gift is from God, but that it still rightfully belongs to Him, is harder to digest. I tried, perhaps unsuccessfully, to explain it to my son this way. When I was a high school student, my parents gave me a car to drive. It was a gift from them, but legally, name on the title, it belonged to them. They gave me some freedom, but as my parents and the car's true owners, they had every right to dictate the use of the car. "Naked I came from my mother's womb, naked I'll return to the womb of the earth. God gives, God takes. God's name ever be blessed," Job 1:21 (MSG).

The first thing He did after creating mankind, "God blessed them," Genesis 1:28a. The last thing Jesus did before leaving this earth and ascending into heaven, "He lifted up his hands and blessed them," Luke 24:50b. No doubt. We are blessed.

Gratitude is the catalyst to being made a blessing. When we recognize how truly blessed we are, we cannot help but give it away. We are compelled to bless in return because we want desperately for other people around us to experience the same blessedness. I challenge you to try counting your blessings. Right now. Grab a napkin, the back of a receipt, a junk mail envelope.... whatever you find handy. Take two minutes to count your blessings, then meet me back here. Scratch down as many things as you can. Aaaand.... Go!

Welcome back. Does your list look anything like mine?

1. Chris, the love of my life
2. Asa, the boy who I "kept bothering" God to send us[2]

3. Porch-sittin' hound dog, Moonshine
4. Nearly-off-grid cabin on the microfarm, home sweet home
5. Ice cream, miracle from milk
6. Plump tomatoes, fresh off the vine, the fruit of my hands
7. Family, by blood or by heart

There is no denying how blessed we are. Documenting our blessings reminds us of just that. Let's keep it up. Start a gratitude journal. Write a new blessing on a chalkboard each day. Post your blessings on social media. Start a blessing blog. Whatever works for you, keep writing it down, counting your blessings. Count everything as a gift from God; there are no small blessings. In fact, when we are able to identify the small things as gifts, as being a blessing to us, then we will recognize the small things we do as being a blessing to others. The larger a gift has to be for us to acknowledge we are blessed, the larger the gift will have to be for us to recognize we are being a blessing. Once we've started, we cannot stop at just the counting. Gratitude shifts our focus to the Blesser and His blessing.

Every November, everywhere we look, we are urged— Give Thanks! The very name of the holiday is a call to action. Thanksgiving! Compelled by friends, we share daily thanks on social media. We artfully sketch poetic lists in gratitude journals. We gather with family 'round tables overflowing with food, and each member takes a turn to voice their gratefulness.

We are encouraged by hearing others express their gratitude, and sharing thankful words of our own reminds us of how truly blessed we are. I was artfully crafting shareable words when I realized: I had forgotten the single most important element. My thanks-giving had morphed into something better described as thanks-stating. You see, stating that I'm thankful is not the same as giving thanks. Sending gratitude out into the universe or even telling my friends how grateful I am for my many blessings, is not the same as saying

"Thank you" to God. I forgot to follow through and express my gratitude to the Giver of the gifts.

Let's keep encouraging one another by sharing all the things we are thankful for. Let's also be intentional about genuinely communicating our thanks to God Himself for every blessing in our lives. Amongst all the stating of thanks, let's be sure to sincerely give thanks to the Giver of every good and perfect gift.

Take a look at the list you made while counting your blessings. Have you taken the time to express your thankfulness to God for all the gifts He's given? If not, make a point to do that today.

"Give thanks to the LORD, for he is good; his love endures forever," 1 Chronicles 16:34.

Blessing Cycle

Why would the Creator of the universe bother to give anything good to us? After God's three-fold declaration of "I will," our part, "you will," finally shows up at the end of the key verse. The reason we are blessed: "*so that* you will be a blessing," (*emphasis mine*). You see, the blessing we receive has a purpose, and it is not what we so often practice. We are not blessed to hoard. (Please don't look in my closets right now and judge me. Although I'm better than I used to be, I am still a work in progress.) We are blessed so that we will be a blessing.

Mom pulled a quarter from the pocket of her black leather purse and pressed it into my open palm. My eyes widened as the gold dish lined with red velvet was passed down the pew toward me. I glanced up beaming as my shiny contribution chimed against the other coins. She did not need my help to put the quarter in; she was completely capable of doing that herself, but my mom was teaching me to give. The quarter was a gift from her, and it belonged to her. She gave me the gift of money, not so I could stuff it into the pocket of my white lace pinafore. I wasn't gifted a quarter to shove in the slot of a gumball machine. It was given to me for the purpose of being given. In the same way, our Daddy in heaven pulls out a blessing and presses it into our lives, so that we will bless someone else. God doesn't need our help, but He is teaching us to give and allowing us the privilege of participating in blessing. Blessing is given to us *so that* we will, in turn, be a blessing.

This Old Testament concept, "I will bless you.... you will be a blessing," is mirrored in the New Testament. Luke 6:38 (NLT) begins, "Give, and you will receive." Bringing these reflective concepts together, we can begin to see a cycle emerge. Travel back with me once again to fifth grade, where in Science class we learned about the water cycle. Evaporation. Condensation. Precipitation. Collection. And then it starts all over again, right? That is what makes it a cycle; it infinitely continues. Just like the water cycle, there is a Blessing Cycle too. You are blessed so that you can bless, and when you give, you will receive. It infinitely continues.

The Blessing Cycle

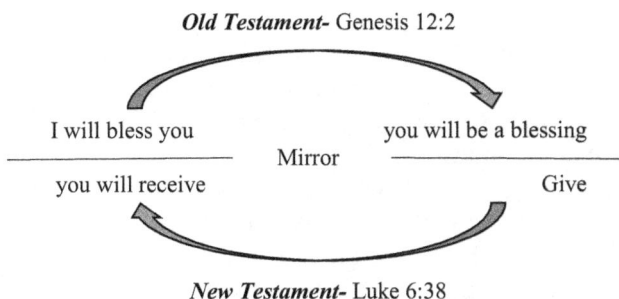

Old Testament- Genesis 12:2

I will bless you   you will be a blessing
                Mirror
you will receive   Give

New Testament- Luke 6:38

"Give, and it will be given to you. A good measure, pressed down, shaken together and running over, will be poured into your lap. For with the measure you use, it will be measured to you," Luke 6:38.

The blessing concept in Luke 6:38 is so often warped, it gets viewed in a Fun House mirror rather than being the reflection of God's heart. Perhaps you have heard this verse quoted along with the promise of a ten-fold return during a donation drive, or in an effort to move you to drop a bigger chunk when the tithe is collected. Although receiving is the promised result of our obedience in giving, it should never be the reason why we give. We must be cautious not to confuse reason and result. Several years ago, I took medication to help me quit smoking, and I also lost weight. Losing weight was not the reason I took the medication, but I did not mind the result.

Let's be clear, blessing others is not a means of securing our own financial and material gain. Receiving is not the end goal of giving. In fact, the exact inverse is true. Giving is the end goal of receiving. I remember a time when I was confused by skewed teaching on this topic. I had been fed a lie, that a blessing a day would keep me healthy, wealthy, and wise. I grinned at the crinkled $10 bill as I placed it in the offering plate on Sunday morning, claiming and fully expecting to receive $100 in return by the end of the week. I was sorely disappointed. We have distorted the gospel if we start viewing the kingdom of God as our own personal short-term investment plan. God's economy will not be reduced to a get-rich-quick scheme. We do not give *so that* we can receive; we receive *so that* we can give. God spoke in Job 41:11, "Who has a claim against me that I must pay? Everything under heaven belongs to me." Make no mistake, God does not owe us a thing. Giving with the motive of gain is not blessing.

When we do bless, the blessing we receive in return may not look anything like the blessing we gave. Blessing may come from an unpredictable direction at an unexpected time. In fact, if we are not diligent in counting our blessings and giving God the credit for every good thing, we may not even notice the blessing when we receive it. We don't have to worry about obtaining blessing. God said He would bless us. It's a promise, and He always keeps His promises. We can trust Him to do His part. We only need to concern ourselves with whether we are doing our part.

Sometimes we are guilty of mistaking blessing as more of a timeline than a cycle. We want to stop at "I will bless you," and "you will receive." We forget about the "you will be a blessing" part, and we skim right past "give." Luke 12:48b says, "From everyone who has been given much, much will be demanded; and from the one who has been entrusted with much, much more will be asked." It is not just nice to pay it forward. As children of God, we are given much, and much is, in fact, required from us. We don't get a high five or a star on our chart for giving back. It is a command. An expectation. A requirement.

Right alongside the give/receive principle, we often talk about Paul's teaching on sowing and reaping. Since starting our little microfarm a few years back, these farming analogies laced throughout Scripture are not lost on me. Of course, farming in the Bible times was not at all like the high-tech operation it is today.

Let's think on the smaller scale of a garden. I drive to the garden center early in spring, buy a few packs of seeds, and plant them in the ground. Although I have tried my hand at seed saving a time or two, for the most part, we eat up all our crop, and I buy new seeds the next spring. There were no big-box discount stores two thousand years ago. Seeds couldn't be ordered with a single mouse click and conveniently shipped overnight directly to your front door. In Bible days, farmers had to do something a little different. They couldn't just thoughtlessly consume their entire harvest; a portion had to be intentionally set aside. Seeds had to be collected for the next year's planting. 2 Corinthians 9:6 says, "Remember this: Whoever sows sparingly will also reap sparingly, and whoever sows generously will also reap generously." This is not simply a metaphorical warning urging us to dig deep in our pockets; it is an agricultural fact. If an adequate supply of seed was not saved back from consumption and sown into the ground, the next harvest would suffer. If the farmer hoarded up all the seed in order to consume it, so fearful to not have enough, that he never sowed a seed again; he would never again receive a harvest or have another seed to sow. A farmer had to prepare in advance and plan ahead to sow generously.

One gardening season when I didn't use up all the seeds I had purchased, I discovered some seeds can go bad. They don't stay potent forever. The longer you hold on to seeds the smaller the harvest will be. I planted those leftover seeds the following year and got less than half of the previous year's yield. We must not be slow in sowing what we have reaped. God does not want our leftovers; He wants our firstfruits.

So you see, blessing is not a timeline with a starting and stopping point. It does not all start with sow, end with reap. The story is not over at harvest time. In fact, quite the opposite is true. Harvest is the very time to intentionally prepare for the next sowing season. We must sow again, so we can reap again, so we can sow again—an ongoing cycle.

Galatians 6:2 tells us to carry each other's burdens. This command must be coupled with the underlying understanding that we should also allow others to bear our burdens. If there were no one allowing, there could be no one carrying. The Blessing Cycle demonstrates being poured into so that we can be poured back out. That means we must also learn and practice the art of gracefully accepting blessing from others. The cycle requires it. If we are never poured into, we will have nothing left to pour out. Every gift is from God, but He uses people to deliver them. When someone else is compelled to give, don't rob them of their opportunity to be a blessing by rejecting their efforts. For many years, I stubbornly refused when a friend offered to pay for coffee. I shot down compliments and deferred encouragement. I declined acts of service, even when I could have really used the help. Through the message of *Make Me a Blessing*, I am slowly learning to receive blessing from others, not begrudgingly, but graciously. I promise it does not come without frequent correction from the Holy Spirit. Allowing someone to bless you, and therefore participate in the Blessing Cycle themselves, can in itself be an act of blessing.

Blessing Packages

I have spent decades of winters shoveling northern Ohio lake-effect snow. While heaving endless shovels of heavier-than-it-looks white powder, I pondered the great mysteries of the universe. Like, how do scientists really know that no two snowflakes are ever the same, because they could not have possibly looked at every single one? I'm sure there's a boring science-y answer to that. Individual blessing opportunities are as numerous and diverse as snowflakes. No more easily cataloged or enumerated, I simply won't try. An effort to make an exhaustive list would be both futile and boring. This one science-y snowflake tidbit I do know. Rather than give each snowflake its own name—Bob, Sally, Ralph, George—scientists have broken them into classifications. That's probably a good idea to do as we dig in to learning about being made a blessing. Gifts come in all shapes and sizes—different packages. Let's sort our blessings into six packages:

Pray. Encourage. Give. Serve. Share. Inspire.

> **Pray**—ask God to meet needs.
> **Encourage**—meet emotional needs.
> **Give**—meet material needs.
> **Serve**—meet physical needs.
> **Share**—meet spiritual needs.
> **Inspire**—compel others to meet needs.

I am brimming with the anticipation of digging deep in the following chapters to unwrap these blessing packages with you!

Circle of Influence

Toddlers thrive on repetition and routine. Thanks to a thoughtful gift from my sister-in-law, and for the love of my boy who was over the moon for her gift, I have watched the animated movie "Robots" about 928 times. Plus one time today for "research." This, by the way, is approximately half as many times as I have enjoyed the classic adventure "The Incredibles." In "Robots," a young robot named Rodney Copperbottom is inspired to invent by his hero Big Weld, a famous inventor. Big Weld strives to make life better for all bots. He advises, "All the tinkering in the world is useless unless it starts with a good idea. So, look around for a need, and start coming up with ideas to fill that need. One idea will lead to another, and before you know it, you've done it. See a need; fill a need."[3]

This is not only good advice for inventing, but it's also a great suggestion for getting started in being made a blessing. See a need; fill a need.

Where do we begin? At the beginning! Our first place of ministry, the epicenter of our circle of influence, is in our homes; right in the place where we live, with our own people. So, we start by seeking to bless our families; each day praying to be a blessing in our homes. Pray for and with our families. Encourage and build them up. Give to our people generously and serve them well. Share God's truth in our homes. Inspire our dear ones to also be a blessing.

I never quite thought of anything I do in my home as being a blessing. After all, I *have* to pray for my family. I *have* to encourage them, give to them, serve them, share with them, and inspire them. It's my sworn duty and obligation as a wife and mother. I signed up for this. Right? Through each of the Blessing Packages, we will see how what we do in our homes and for our families really does make a difference.

"We instructed you how to live in order to please God, as in fact you are living. Now we ask you and urge you in the Lord Jesus to do this more and more," 1 Thessalonians 4:1b. Paul assured the Thessalonian church, they were already doing a great job and urged them to keep on keepin' on. I hope to relay that same message to you. In our time together, my heart is to help you understand and acknowledge—you are already blessing in more ways than you realize. And to encourage you—continue to be a blessing, more and more.

Four authors, four locations, four decades. God breathed, and words flowed from the ends of four pens. Matthew. Mark. Luke. John. At first glance, all four men appear to have written the same story. Why not combine? Why not write just one Gospel? I'll answer that question with a corny joke. What do a Jewish tax collector, a missionary companion of Paul, a Gentile physician, and the disciple who Jesus loved, all have in common? You know the punch line. They each wrote one of the Gospels. What is important is what they don't have in common. Perspective. Voice. Audience. Circle of influence. In fact, when you read closely, the Gospels are not redundant at all. Where human understanding would say, "It has already been written. That role has been filled. There are enough of those." God says, "For my thoughts are not your thoughts, neither are your ways my ways," Isaiah 55:8. Who He uses and how He uses them may not add up on paper. That's good news for those of us crying out, "Make me a blessing." God will not say, "That position has been filled." He has a good plan to use each of us!

Just like the Gospel writers, God wants to use you. Your position has not already been filled. You are not redundant. You have a unique perspective, voice, audience, and circle of influence. God has placed each person in a distinct environment—where you live, where you work, where you travel, where you grocery shop, and where you stop to pick up dinner on the way home from the grocery store because you are too tired to cook after having just spent $200 on food. We each have an individual opportunity to bless a specific someone that no one else may have. In your home, in your workplace, in your church, in your community. See a need; fill a need.

How do we determine our circle of influence? I am a nerd for mnemonic devices. (Little tricks to help you remember things. Like "Roy G Biv" to recall the colors of the rainbow: red, orange, yellow, green, blue, indigo, violet.) In fact, in my writing journal, I have written the phrase "I <3 alliteration" at least five times. This time we'll use the acronym FRANKS to identify our circle of influence.

Friends. Relatives. Acquaintances. Neighbors. Kids' Connections. Strangers.

Friends—people we like, enjoy, and choose to spend our time with.
Relatives—people we are connected to legally by blood, adoption, marriage.
Acquaintances—people we know by name at work, organizations, church.
Neighbors—people within our local community.
Kids' Connections—people we see at our children's events and activities.
Strangers—people who we happen upon irregularly in our daily lives.

Your home, your family, your immediate circle of influence does not look exactly like mine. But rest assured. God has you right where He wants you. He will use you in ways that will astonish you if you are willing to make yourself available to be used in the Blessing Cycle.

Fad Diet

Please tell me I'm not alone; maybe you've experienced this too. When I have decided to "get fit," perhaps for the 100th time, I "commit" to working hard for a week or two. But the minute I drop a few pounds (or worse, when I have given up because I have not lost any) I head straight back to the donuts. Throughout my life, I have tried what seems like every "fad diet" that's come along. The grapefruit diet. The cabbage soup diet. Those shakes that taste like liquid sidewalk chalk. I even made up my own crazy green bean diet. Let me explain. My brother's dog was significantly overweight, and the veterinarian prescribed a green bean diet. By substituting her regular food for green beans, she was back in young pup shape in no time. I figured if it worked for the Golden Retriever, why wouldn't it work for me? Consequently, I decided to go on the green bean diet. I even talked a few of my co-workers into joining me. The four of us agreed to eat nothing but green beans, every meal, for an entire week. The first morning, we all sat in our shared office, noses turned up, choking down green beans for breakfast. By 10 am I had given up. Cathy caught me red-handed at the vending machine—an icy-cold Coke clenched in one fist and a Milky Way Dark in the other.

To be honest, I've tried my fair share of "Spiritual Fad Diets" too. I am not talking about a literal, nutritional change from a Christian perspective. You know what I mean, right? Pray this prayer, quote this verse, or make these six statements every day, and your life will be transformed. These things were good and did produce fruit, but they were only sustainable until the next thing came along. We can't do everything. Something's got to give. So I let the last lesson slide in order to embrace the next one.

We all know true, sustainable physical transformation does not come in the form of a fad diet or a magic pill. It only comes from lifestyle change. This same principle of "a lifestyle, not a diet," applies directly to embracing the message of *Make Me a Blessing.*

Some things are only for a season, but not this message. Being made a blessing is not a feel-good story to pick up and put back on the shelf once it's done the job of entertaining us. We cannot put this lesson down and be on to the next thing. This is *the* thing. Well, it's the second thing anyway. Jesus said the whole gospel can be summed up in two things. Love God. Love others (Matthew 22:37-40). *Make Me a Blessing* is the call to action produced by love for others. The reason we love others is to point them to Jesus. You see, we are not all called to full-time ministry, but we are all called to full-time Christianity.

While we won't dig deep into the command to love, love is the undercurrent carrying us through every concept we'll explore together. 1 John 3:18 says, "Dear children, let us not love with words or speech but with actions and in truth." *Make Me a Blessing* zones in on the practical application—the activity of demonstrating God's love to others. The Bible makes it clear that it is possible for us to love without blessing[4] and to bless without loving.[5] Paul tells us in Romans 12:9a, "Love must be sincere." As we dig into what it looks like to be made a blessing, let's make this the prayer of our hearts:

Lord, make my love sincere, for my family, for my friends, for everyone in my circle of influence.

I do not want to go away from this lesson unchanged, and I pray you don't either. This is not a Christian fad diet. Being made a blessing is not about checking a box. It is not doing a good deed for the day. This is about a change of heart that causes us to look outside ourselves—day by day—moment by moment. Hands open to God, begging for opportunities to fulfill our purpose, to be made a blessing. Looking at each person we encounter as the potential recipient of the many gifts with which we have been entrusted. The heart of blessing is having a heart to bless.

A diet is a conscious effort to temporarily restrict or force behavior. A lifestyle is an unconscious action that has become a permanent part of who we are. I get in the car and put on my seatbelt. I don't even think about it. I reach back, pull forward, and click in one fluid motion. Without ever giving it a second thought. With consistent practice, intentional becomes instinctual. That is how readily I want blessing to flow from me.

I pray we experience a lifestyle change, a cry of our hearts, a soul-deep reformation. Oh, friend, that we would come away from our time together looking different on the inside. So different, that we can never again allow ourselves to go back to the way we were. My hope is that we would have the words "Make me a blessing" branded on our souls and emblazoned on our hearts, as an inseparable part of who we are. Permanent. We cannot help but bless because it is so ingrained in our behavior that it just oozes out. Unconscious. Blessing no longer has to be premeditated. It just happens, and we don't even realize until later. "Hey, I blessed someone today!" Even better, someone thanks us for being a blessing, and we have no idea what they're talking about because God simply answered our prayer, "Make me a blessing."

CHAPTER 2

To Don't List

In 1955, a 14-year-old boy was dragged from his home in the middle of the night and brutally murdered because of the color of his skin. The man who later openly admitted to this atrocity was acquitted by a jury of his peers. I wept bitterly reading the horrific details describing the torture of this child, who was just barely older than my own boy. I wept for his fear and the pain he endured, for his sweet mama who would never hold him again. How could any person have such hate, such disregard for the life of another human being? How could no one speak up? I wept because this was surely only one story with hundreds, maybe thousands like it untold. I cried out, "Dear God, what do I do with this?"

I don't usually read this kind of story. I just keep scrolling. I think most of us just keep scrolling, and it's not limited to our screens. We switch the channel; we flip the page; we turn our heads; we keep on walking. Why do we look the other way? We keep scrolling when we see horrific stories of the past because we want to believe it happened a long time ago, that things are different now. Actually, 60 some years is not so long ago. Looking back at the Fifties we think of the good old days. When families sat together at the dinner table, and children played outside after dark. Stores were closed on

Sunday. People knew their neighbors and left their doors unlocked. While it is true, things are different now, different does not mean better. We cannot honestly believe people are nicer and kinder these days—that the world is a better place. The Bible prophesies of increased wickedness.[1] In fact, in the last 60 years, we have experienced significant moral decline. "Anyone who hates a brother or sister is a murderer," according to 1 John 3:15a. How people express their hate is sometimes different today than in times past, but we still have a world full of hate.

We keep scrolling when we see current day atrocities because we don't think we can do anything to help. There are real problems in the world today. Big problems. Starvation. Human trafficking. Disaster. Genocide. Oppression. I mean, we want to be a blessing, but where would we even start? The problems seem too big; our contributions seem too small. "What could I possibly do?" We ask the question rhetorically and keep scrolling because we could not bear to hear an answer. What if we took time to ponder that question instead of moving on so quickly? What if we didn't just ask ourselves, but we ask Someone who actually knows the answer? The truth is, we are right. We cannot do much in our own strength. What if we ask the only One who could empower us to make a difference? When we limit the solution to what we can do, we are not only limiting ourselves, we are limiting God.

We keep scrolling when we see problems big and small because, honestly, we don't want to know; we don't want to be bothered. In Jesus' story about the Good Samaritan, both the priest and the Levite kept scrolling. I remember handing a friend one of my favorite books about a woman who overcame tragedy. My friend said, "Why would I want to read about her problems? I have enough of my own."

We are content to be blissfully unaware of pain and suffering. We want to keep believing the world is a mostly nice place, full of mostly good people. If we believe anything to the contrary, we may feel compelled to do something about it. Of course, there is a balance to be had. If we focus all our attention on the bad in the world, we will never leave our beds or pull the covers from our heads. Philippians 4:8 tells us to dwell on what is true, noble, right, pure, lovely, and admirable. We also need frequent reminders that we are living in a dark, broken world. Our eyes have to be opened to the hurting around us. We must see needs in order to fill needs.

There are a million excuses for why we keep scrolling. We don't have money; we don't have time. We keep scrolling because we forget—all that we are and all that we have is a gift from God and belongs to God.

All our scrolling excuses have the same origin—self-focus. Self-focus is the #1 enemy of blessing. Selfishness is epidemic, ingrained in our DNA. The very first sin was self-indulgent. In fact, all sin, darkness, and evil are rooted in one thing: the sickness of self. It is a disease every one of us enters the world carrying. "The moment you have a self at all, there is a possibility of putting yourself first—wanting to be the centre—wanting to be God, in fact." –C.S. Lewis[2]

We are born selfish. With our first gasp, we breathe in atmosphere and breathe out self. A newborn cries. Change me. Feed me. Hold me. An infant has no concern for anyone but herself. As we grow more, we want more. The truth is, without intervention, it is not much better for us as adults. We worship the trinity of me, myself, and I. The sickness of self is so prevalent in our society, we no longer recognize it as a disease. Instead, we celebrate it, encourage it, spread it.

Self-help. Self-affirmation. Self magazine. Selfies.

If we want to be effective in blessing, we must get over our-*self*. Self-focus blinds us to the needs around us and keeps us from blessing. In "Mary Poppins," Burt comments that Mr. Banks "can't see past the end of his nose."[3] As children, we laughed and went cross-eyed trying to reproduce what Mr. Banks saw. Every day, we miss countless opportunities to bless because we are so consumed with our own problems, we can't see past the ends of our noses. We can't see the fields of needs around us, for the corn stalk of our own lives. We just keep scrolling. I would be horrified to know exactly how many opportunities I have missed.

My head had been throbbing all morning; by lunchtime, I was sick to my stomach. On our way for a quick bite, we drove past a filthy, straggle-haired man with a sign in hand. "Disabled Veteran. Anything will help." My eyes avoided contact as my head turned the other direction; I could not think about that. I hurt too much to care. A few bites settled my stomach, and I remembered the man I disregarded earlier. Did I miss the opportunity to bless him? From the restaurant window, I couldn't see if he was still at the corner. I asked my husband to buy a to-go meal for the man anyway; the possibility was worth five bucks. We rounded the block, relieved to see the man still standing in the same spot. "God bless you," he said, reaching for the brown paper bag. I choked up. "Thanks for serving. I'll be praying for you." Those were all the words I could muster. The man scurried back to his spot, tore into the bag, and started shoving fries in his mouth, hand after hand. That is what hunger looks like. Hunger is not, "It's noon o' five, and I haven't had a morsel since breakfast."

I thank God for the opportunity to bless, but even more so, for the lesson to stop scrolling. I almost missed this opportunity for wallowing in self-pity. When we are hurting, physically or emotionally, self-absorption is multiplied. We do need to care for ourselves; we do need to heal. We also need to be aware of the tendency to become so consumed with ourselves that we block out everyone else. God continues to put opportunities in our paths. When we are hurting, we need to be all the more intentional about meeting the needs around us. Not a reason to bless, but the result of blessing just may be some relief from our hurt.

Others-Focus

"Then God said, 'Let us make mankind in our image, in our likeness,'" Genesis 1:26a. When God looks into the face of every human being on this planet, He sees His own reflection. That is how He wants us to see other people too. No one is less important, less human, less valuable, less loved. Not every person is a child of God, but He longs for them to be. "He doesn't want anyone lost," 2 Peter 3:9b (MSG). It's easier to keep scrolling if we don't see people as co-creation, if we don't look them in the eye.

For days, the article I normally would have scrolled past continued to press heavy on my heart. "Lord, what do I do with this ache? I want to stop scrolling. I want to truly see people as You see them. I want to look people in the eye, and see Your face in their faces." It starts by approaching each person, each interaction praying, "How can I show them Your love? How can I be a blessing?" Receiving blessing that we do not deserve is the definition of grace. "How can I give grace to this person with the face of God?"

The next time I ran errands, I resolved not to scroll past people. I put my phone away and gave my undivided attention. I looked each person in the eye and thought, "God's face. Give grace." My smile could not be contained as I thought it. The librarian, "God's face. Give grace." I was compelled to show her gratitude. The clerk at the post office, "God's face. Give grace." I asked her name and called her by it as I said, "Have a good day." The checkout girl who double charged me, "God's face. Give grace." I assured her we all make mistakes. It sounds small, but it's a huge step toward overcoming self-focus and becoming others-focused. This approach connects us to the heart of God for the hearts of people. When we look someone in the eye and think, "God's face. Give grace." It will be harder to judge, harder to criticize, harder to keep scrolling. But that's not all. It will be easier to care, easier to love, easier to bless. By living others-focused lives of blessing, we are saying, "You are made in the image of God, and He loves you!"

To Don't List

It turns out, just like snowflakes and opportunities to bless, there are countless ways to NOT be a blessing. Hang in here with me while I share a few stories of (mostly my own) blessing fails. Most of our failures in an effort to bless are the result of self-focus. There are three indicators that we are self-centered in our attempts to be a blessing. Ego—How does blessing affect me? Expectations—What am I owed in return for blessing? Earning—What's in it for me if I bless? Each indicator can be broken down into specific things we don't want to do—a To Don't List.

Ego: Don't Be Obligated

I love to do good things when I feel so inclined, but the moment anything is mandated, my teeth clench. Open hands ball into tight little fists. Paul told the Corinthians not to give "under compulsion."[4] But we can't always prevent being coerced into giving an obligatory "gift" or forced to "volunteer" for a cause we don't care about. Adult life comes with many responsibilities we would not sign up for if we got to pick. We might be asked to donate cash to buy a Christmas present for the boss we really don't like. Every parent on the team may be automatically drafted to work concessions at the ball game. If we cannot avoid these situations, how do we guard against blessing out of obligation? It all comes down to one thing. Attitude. Remember, the heart of blessing is having a heart to bless. We cannot always choose our circumstances, but we can choose the way we look at them. We can pout, stomp, and grumble. Or we can remember, all that we are and all that we have is a gift from God and belongs to Him. We can thank God for the opportunity to be a blessing. Ask Him to reveal the good He has planned, even if it is not how we would have planned it. The good news is, even our obligations can be redeemed; they can do a 180-degree turn and become blessings with a change of attitude.

Ego: Don't Feel Superior

"Terrible parents," Bev ranted. She was disgusted by her neighbors' grubby kids. Their ill-fitting clothes were always mismatched if they were wearing any clothes at all. Bev cleaned out her children's closets and gave the neighbors her discards to ensure those scoundrels would have something decent to wear.

This reminds me of the Pharisee in Luke 18:9-14 who prayed loudly in the street. "God, I thank you that I am not like other people." He proceeded to list their faults and his virtues. None of us should ever think we are better than anyone else. Philippians 2:3 says, "Do nothing out of selfish ambition or vain conceit. Rather, in humility value others above yourselves." A true giver is not self-centered, critical, and condescending. A heart to bless will have compassion for the person in need.

Ego: Don't Complain

Patty fumed at length about her friend's move. She drove nearly an hour to the friend's home, only to find not a single belonging was ready to go. Nothing was packed. There were no newspapers to wrap fragile pieces and no boxes to pack things. The two ladies picked up a few items, less than a carload, and drove to the new place. Patty's friend showed her around, unpacked the half load, then whittled away two hours just talking. Patty left in a huff. This friend, under the guise of needing help, wasted away her entire day.

Patty did not know; her friend had lost her dream home to foreclosure. She was overwhelmed by the idea of packing up everything she owned and moving to the modest, all she could afford, rental home. What Patty's friend needed was not someone to help put things into boxes and carry them across town. She needed someone to help put her heart back together, help her carry the heavy load of disappointment.

When we offer to help, there may be a deeper need than we perceive. We must be flexible, listening, in order to meet real needs. I often tell my son, "Helping is not only doing what's fun; it's doing whatever needs to be done."

"With their mouths they bless, but in their hearts they curse," Psalm 62:4b. That is the same two-faced thing we do when we complain about the people we have "blessed." God is not surprised by anything we encounter. He knows in advance how our opportunities will turn out. He has a specific purpose for our participation, even if we do not understand it.

Ego: Don't Brag

During our time together, I will share many examples of how God has allowed me and other people to be a blessing. Isn't that wrong? After all, the Bible tells us to let our giving be done in secret.[5] I believe we can learn from each other's experiences. Blessing is not intuitive to everyone. I would have never considered bringing a meal to a new mom until a friend talked about having done so. My cousin, Aaron, shares his experiences helping homeless people. Before I heard Aaron's stories, I kept scrolling when I saw a homeless person on the street corner. It's not that I didn't care, but it's awkward. I hoped the light would turn green before I made eye contact. But because of my cousin's example, I started to reach out instead of driving by. Hearing other people's blessing experiences can encourage and inspire us. There is a distinct difference between sharing an illustration for the purpose of edification and sharing to get a pat on the back.

One sign of sharing for illustration is making general and anonymous statements. Being overly specific can seem like bragging. Telling names of people we helped, sharing generous dollar amounts (including conveniently leaving price tags on expensive items), expressing how hard we worked, or how much we sacrificed sounds like bragging. Humility is essential in being a blessing.

Ego: Don't Take Rejection Personally

Jesus was perfect, blameless, and sinless. Still, people rejected Him. He assures us, they will reject us too. But don't take it personally.

I hate to see anything go to waste. Except for a few special keepsakes, I give my child's clothes and toys away as soon as he outgrows them. My son made a new, younger friend, and I saw an opportunity to bless. Every visit, I sent the boy home with something. One day at pick up, the boy's dad said, "You can stop sending your junk to my house."

I'm not sure if I was more hurt or offended. I thought I was doing something good. Some of my favorite things as a child were hand-me-downs from my older cousins. It was an honor, and I wore their name-brand clothes like a medal. I guess the dad did not see it that way. I could speculate what the reasons may have been, but I don't really know why. Jesus told His disciples, when they faced rejection, "Shrug your shoulders and move on," Luke 9:5 (MSG).

I found someone new to bless with my son's gently used treasures. A postcard a few weeks later shared a little boy's joy over his new treasures and his mom's gratitude. When that boy grew, the gifts were passed on to the single mom next door with two boys even younger. I could have been so offended by rejection that I decided to stop giving altogether. Instead, I "shrugged my shoulders and moved on" to bless someone else. Moving on scored me a front row seat to the Blessing Cycle in action. I was blessed so I could be a blessing. The family I blessed, was able to bless once more. Know that God sees our efforts even when people do not appreciate them. He has a good plan to use us to bless.

Expectations: Don't Expect Reciprocation

I recently read a social media post by someone who is "always helping other people, always giving, always serving, but no one ever serves or gives to him." While I was annoyed by his tirade, the truth is, I can identify. I just wouldn't say it out loud in public. After all, isn't it reasonable? If we are constantly helping other people, can't we expect them to help us when we need it? In the last chapter, didn't we learn we should accept blessing from others?

My husband, Chris, has a knack for all sorts of guy things, and his aptitude makes him the doer of many favors. I wish I could tell you I have always been grateful that he was being a blessing. Regrettably, I have thrown my fair share of pity parties because my project list suffered as he helped someone else. Chris was happy to assist the Holy Spirit in correcting my attitude. I eventually accepted that my husband was serving with his gifts.

One weekend, my husband and I, along with our son, were installing fence around our pasture. Digging post holes, by hand, in solid clay soil, is hard physical labor. Just the three of us were quickly drenched in sweat and out of breath. I wondered out loud, "Where are all of our helpers?" Surely of the many people my husband had often lent a hand, someone could pitch in here. My husband was not amused by my comment.

When one of the frequent favor askers stopped by, I thought for sure he was there to assist. He shot the breeze for a few minutes and took off. I spouted, "He didn't even offer to help?" Chris sent a glare in my direction, and I knew enough to shut my mouth, but the conversation continued in my head. "After all the weekends and late nights my husband has spent helping him, he couldn't even pick up a shovel?"

My husband helped without expectation, so he was not taken aback by failure to reciprocate. He helps because he can, because he is blessed with a great many talents. He does not mind sharing his gifts, even when I think he should hoard them.

Sun peaked through the changing leaves, enticing my twenty-something self out for an afternoon stroll. I smiled at the wrinkled stranger who was working a rake and gathering a jump-worthy pile. The neighborhood was quiet, except for the rustling leaves, until the old man hollered, "You know, you could help!" I darted the city block back to my garage and soon located my own wood-handled leaf-pile-maker. You won't believe it when I tell you; the man I met, out raking his own lawn, was 103 years old. I didn't believe it either, but he had a driver's license to prove it. The thought had not crossed my mind to pitch in when I saw the elderly man doing yardwork, but I was happy to help at my neighbor's request. Blessing is not intuitive to everyone. Just like me and my husband's favor-asking friend, not everyone will recognize your need. If you need help, ask.

In the Blessing Cycle, we talked about accepting blessing from others. That is *accept*, not *expect*. In fact, Jesus tells us to give to those who cannot repay.[6] When we bless, we don't know the direction from which we will be blessed in return. The blessing we receive may look nothing like the blessing we give. Rest assured the Source of the giving is always the same. God often uses people in the delivery, but He is always the One doing the blessing. God will supply all our needs. It's a promise. He may or may not choose to bless us through the same someone He used us to bless. In addition, not everyone is participating in the Blessing Cycle. The promise, "I will bless you, so that you will be a blessing," was to Abraham and his descendants. Remember Galatians 3:29, "If you belong to Christ, then you are Abraham's seed, and heirs according to the promise." A person can do good deeds all day long, but if they haven't accepted Jesus as their Savior, the commands and the promises in God's Word do not apply to them. That means we cannot expect them to abide by the same rules.

Direct reciprocation can turn into a "scratch my back and I'll scratch yours" scenario that has us leaving God completely out of the equation. We can start to depend on our own works or the reliability of others to meet our needs, instead of looking to God as the Giver of every good thing.

Expectations: Don't Expect Gratitude

We talked about counting our blessings and being thankful to God, and later we will discuss showing gratitude to others who bless us. When we learn a lesson, it is difficult not to think everyone else ought to do the same. Shouldn't we be able to expect just a little gratitude in return? After all, we sacrifice our time and resources. Is a "Thank you" too much to ask?

If we have a child, grandchild, trainee, mentee, student—anyone whose character development is entrusted to us—by all means, we should teach and expect gratitude. If we don't get thanks, we need to correct it immediately. I often nudge children, "I didn't hear anyone say, 'Thank you.'" This is actually our job; we are commissioned to point those in our care to proper behavior.

Let's be honest, most of the time, the gratitude we are expecting is not in these overseer situations. We are not in charge of the character of the world at large. We have no right to expect thanks or correct lack of it. In fact, not everyone has learned gratitude or how to express it.

A servant's heart is difficult to maintain when you feel taken for granted or underappreciated. While we need to know where to draw the line so we are not taken advantage of, we also have to keep in mind the reason we bless. It's not for appreciation, it's for the glory of God.

A gust of arctic air blew my stack of papers from the restaurant counter. I called in my mother voice to my employee, Amy, who was about to walk home. "It's freezing outside! Where's your coat?" She shrugged. I rushed to the back room and grabbed the coat I had worn that day. Brown corduroy with faux lamb's wool lining. I obviously had an attachment to that coat, since at this very moment I can still imagine nestling in it. I had other jackets, honestly, more than I needed. I presented the coat like a prize. She threw it on and scurried out the door.

The selfless act made me smile; I had just made my day. As I hustled to my car, shivering that evening, I patted myself on the back all the more, remembering what a great sacrifice I had made. The next day, Amy trudged in donning my snuggly brown gift. I grinned sheepishly, making eye contact for an awkwardly long time, and cheered, "Good morning!" She shrugged. I waited out the busy day. At quitting time, there was a similar lack of exchange. I bristled a bit, "A 'Thank you' would have been nice." Time went by. Some frigid days, Amy was not even wearing my beloved coat. Once, she had the audacity to march through the door in some ugly yellow puffy excuse for a jacket. Ugh! She didn't even need my coat! She had one all along and was simply too irresponsible to put it on the day I had been duped into giving her mine. She never even said so much as a "Thanks." She could at least offer to give it back!

I am embarrassed to share this story. More embarrassed that there were many more times I have begrudged giving something that went unappreciated or underutilized. Sadly, I was expecting gratitude but wasn't freely giving it at the time. Luke 6:35 says, "But love your enemies, do good to them, and lend to them *without expecting to get anything back.* Then your reward will be great, and you will be children of the Most High, because he is kind to the *ungrateful* and wicked," (*emphasis mine*).

Oh dear, that verse points an arrow straight at my heart. I look back at my Count Your Blessings List, convicted of how ungrateful I have been. I have failed to acknowledge every single thing as a gift from Him, and I have surely neglected to express gratitude for all of it. I had not thanked God for the warm snugglefest of a jacket. I saw it. I wanted it. I purchased it. I wore it. I. I. I. I. Not once did I acknowledge God. How dare I expect gratitude when I have been so negligent in giving it?

We not only expect gratitude, we are pretty sure there is an acceptable level of gratitude. A simple "Thank you" may not suffice if our sacrifice was sizeable. We may expect a card, the occasional billboard, or perhaps eternal servitude. Is bowing too much to ask?

The glory and the gratitude belong to God. So even when we receive gratitude, we should deflect it to Him. Not as one of those annoyingly saintly people who refuse to let you appreciate them at all. Don't expect. Do accept. The reason we bless, our motivation has to be for the glory of God. But other good things will come to us as the result of our obedience in being a blessing. It's the Blessing Cycle. There may be times when we are recognized and appreciated for our good work. A gracious "You're welcome," and acceptance of appreciation is not out of order. We must let other people pour into us. False humility, or completely refusing to accept anything in return, can be frustrating to someone else who is trying to be a blessing to us.

Earning: Don't Try to Buy Happiness

It feels good to do good. I won't bore you with a science-y fact about endorphins or a chemical reaction in our brains that causes the good feeling. If we are trying to feel good about ourselves through blessing, we are seeking our worth from the wrong source. God is our joy; He wants our happiness to be found in Him alone. This is another example of reason versus result. We will not find happiness if it is the reason for our good works. However, when we begin to see God working through us and allowing us to participate in His Blessing Cycle, we will find a joy that cannot be contained as a result.

Likewise, if we are only giving to make someone else happy, thinking the gift given will be a source of joy, we are giving in the wrong spirit. Lives cannot be permanently changed by a change of circumstance, only by a change of heart. We bless to point others to Jesus. He will give them true joy beyond any temporary good feeling we can offer. Others will not find what they need if they are seeking joy from our blessing. When our blessing points people to Jesus, they will find everlasting joy.

Earning: Don't Try to Buy God's Love

We may think our good deeds will catch God's eye and earn us a spot in heaven. There is nothing we can do to earn God's love or forgiveness. It is freely offered to us. But we do know, nothing in life is free. Just because you or I don't have to pay for it, does not mean it is without cost. Salvation of our souls comes at a great price.

Here is what the Bible says about being saved:

Romans 3:23 "for all have sinned and fall short of the glory of God." Without arguing about what you think is sin compared to what I think is sin, if we are honest with ourselves, each of us would admit we have sinned. We have lied or cheated or stolen or gossiped. We have fallen short of the perfect standard of God.

Romans 6:23 "For the wages of sin is death, but the gift of God is eternal life in Christ Jesus our Lord." There is a price to pay for sin. Justice demands punishment. That punishment is eternity separated from God in a literal hell. But God offers the free gift of salvation. There is nothing we can do to be good enough. The gift of God is given through Jesus Christ, who is not one way, He is the only way.

Romans 5:8 "But God demonstrates his own love for us in this: While we were still sinners, Christ died for us." God loves us so much, that He sent His son Jesus to pay the penalty for our sin. Jesus took our punishment in His death on the cross. We don't have to clean ourselves up first. We can come to Him just as we are.

Romans 10:9 "If you declare with your mouth, 'Jesus is Lord,' and believe in your heart that God raised him from the dead, you will be saved." It seems too simple, doesn't it? We think we need to subscribe to a certain religion or follow a specific set of rules to be saved. That is not the case. We must repent—acknowledge we are sinners—and understand there is a price to pay. We know we cannot be good enough or pay the debt on our own. We must believe God sent His only Son Jesus to pay the price for our sin. He rose again so we could be in relationship with the Father. All we have to do is accept the free gift of salvation and confess—make Jesus the Lord, or Authority, over our lives.

All it takes is a simple heartfelt prayer, not something complicated, no magic words. Just a conversation, one on One, between you and your Creator God. If you are ready to make that decision about your eternity, you can pray this simple prayer along with me, or pray words of your own.

God, I acknowledge I am a sinner, and I repent of my sin. I understand justice demands my sins be punished. I cannot pay the price or be good enough to reconcile that. Thank You for sending Your Son Jesus in my place, to pay the wages for my sin. He rose again so I could have relationship with You. I accept Your free gift of salvation. I confess Jesus as the Lord; I make Him the Authority over my life. Thank you for saving me. In Jesus' name, amen.

Romans 10:13 "for, 'Everyone who calls on the name of the Lord will be saved.'" If you prayed that prayer or one like it with sincerity in your heart, you will be saved!

God's unconditional love is a difficult thing for us to wrap our minds around, because we love conditionally, because we have been loved conditionally. Even after we have already accepted the free gift of salvation, it may still be difficult to truly grasp that we cannot, or do not need to work for the love of our Father. The fact that we cannot earn anything from God is true not only of salvation. He never loves you more or less. His love is constant and unconditional. "I have loved you with an everlasting love," Jeremiah 31:3b.

We know we do not bless *so that* we can be blessed. We bless *because* we have been blessed. In the same way, we do not bless *so that* we can be loved. We are already loved, unconditionally, by the Creator of the Universe. We bless *because* we are loved. When we grab hold of the truth that we are loved by God, we cannot help but show other people the same love in return. Thank God we aren't expected to earn His love or favor, we'd fall short every time. We bless because we already have the love and favor of our Father. God does not love us because of our works, but because of God's unmerited love, we are motivated to do good works.

Overcoming the Sickness of Self

I must confess, I have practiced every item on the To Don't list. That's how I know about them. If you have identified with any or all of the self-centered indicators, take heart. There is a cure for the sickness of self.

Let's soak in the words of John 3:30 in several translations:

"He must become greater; I must become less." (NIV)
"He must become more important. I must become less important." (NLV)
"He must become greater and greater, and I must become less and less." (NLT)
"He must increase, but I must decrease." (NASB)
"This is the assigned moment for him to move into the center, while I slip off to the sidelines." (MSG)
In my own words: "MORE HE. less me."

Less Me

As long as we are filled with self, there is no room for anyone else, including God. There is not room to be full of the Holy Spirit if I am already full of me. I cannot have outward effectiveness with inward focus.

Jesus said, "Whoever wants to be my disciple must deny themselves and take up their cross daily and follow me," Luke 9:23. What does denying ourselves look like? Talking about self-discipline in 1 Corinthians 9, Paul says, "I do not run like someone running aimlessly; I do not fight like a boxer beating the air. No, I strike a blow to my body." We can't take this lightly. If we are serious about conquering our self-obsession, we have to beat down our flesh. It is not a one and done experience. Every single day we need to hand ourselves over to our Creator.

"Now repentance is no fun at all. It is much harder than merely eating humble pie. It means unlearning all the self-conceit and self-will that we have been training ourselves into for thousands of years. It means killing yourself, undergoing a kind of death." –C.S. Lewis[7]

While studying self-denial, I wanted to give it a try. I gave something up one day and talked myself into overindulging the next. It takes six weeks to build or break a habit. God already knew this little tidbit before researchers discovered it. In fact, it was His design. Only, maybe the researchers were a couple of days off. Among many other 40-day illustrations in the Bible, Jesus set the example by fasting for 40 days.[8] (That's awfully close to six weeks.)

The rains and floods continued for 40 days as the evil on the earth was wiped out.[9] Perhaps it could take 40 days to wipe out our habit of self-service. To the Jews, 40 days meant a time of trial or probation. Maybe that's just what our flesh needs, to be put on probation.

We have to stop being pushed around by self-interest. In fact, when our flesh tries to tell us what to do, we need to put our hands on our hips, stick out our tongues and shout, "You're not the boss of me!" I knew I had to add structure and commitment to self-denial so I wasn't "beating into the air." For self-denial to be effective in striking a blow to our bodies it must be:

Prayed. Personal. Precise. Painful. Partnered.

Prayed: We cannot approach sacrifice flippantly. I always want to jump in and do the first thing that pops into my head. That may not be reasonable or effective. We need dedicated time in prayer asking God to tell us how we can best deny ourselves.

Personal: For each of us it will be different. I probably do not struggle with the same issues you do. Self-denial must be something I am giving up, not following someone else's lead or imposing on the people around me. When I was giving up desserts, I did not force that on my family. When I made them brownies, and I abstained, now that was sacrifice.

Precise: Our self-sacrifice has to be specific. Vague statements like "Eat better" leave us open to pig out on cupcakes because we ate a salad for lunch. "Go to bed and get up earlier" isn't clear enough. We should choose one well-defined thing to deny.

Painful: Sacrifice has to be, well, sacrificial. We have to give up something that hurts a little bit, something we like, maybe even love. If we find it easy, it's probably not much of a sacrifice. Giving up Brussels sprouts is not a sacrifice for me. Remember, we are beating down our flesh here. It will not feel good at first, it may even be painful. I have to let go of something I'm actually going to miss in order to make it a blow to my body.

Partnered: We need accountability. It is easy to talk myself out of something when no one else knows. But the minute I have shared my commitment, it seems somehow more solidified. This does not mean we need to partner with someone on the same journey. I messaged my friend, "I'm giving up sugar for 40 days. Will you please hold me accountable?" She prayed for me from time to time and checked in once or twice. Another time I shared with my small group that I would be signing off of social media for a season. That's all we need, to know someone else knows and is in our corner rooting for us.

I started out small, but not small to me. It actually began seemingly by accident, but we know nothing really happens that way. I was at home for a week after Christmas, when I realized I had not had a Coca-Cola in seven days. I decided I could kick that habit once and for all, so I committed it to God for 40 days. Just because we do not plan it or start under God's authority, does not mean we cannot submit it to Him. If you have never had an addiction to soda pop, you may not get it.

For me, 40 days was a big deal! Friend, I kid you not, several nights during that time of sacrifice, I literally had dreams about sipping an icy-cold Coke. That may be a tell-tale sign I had a problem.

I continued to add 40 days, changing up what I would sacrifice. I wondered if what I gave up this time was silly. The moment I hit "send" on the message asking my friend to keep me accountable, the walls began to close in, and my pounding heart was only muffled by my gasping for air. Could I really do this? Forty days is a long time. I was familiar with this feeling; I had this exact sensation when God instructed me to let go of an idol several years earlier. That was the moment I knew for sure, I had to overcome this thing. "What people value highly is detestable in God's sight," Luke 16:15b. If there is something we think we could never give up, we could not live without, it may just be an idol. Anything we value too highly becomes detestable to God.

We usually start something new at the beginning of the year, the first of the month, the start of the week. A clean page for a clean slate. Maybe we wait to give something up for Lent. Don't put this off! We can't wait for the calendar to change before we do. Even if we make a few missteps, every time we say "No" to our self and "Yes" to Jesus, we grow weaker in our flesh and stronger in our spirit!

More He

Denying ourselves—less me—is a vital part, of conquering the sickness of self, but not the entire equation. The other factor is more of Him. "I have been crucified with Christ and I no longer live, but Christ lives in me," Galatians 2:20a. We need to be empty of ourselves, so we can be full of Him. Moses spent 40 days with the Lord on the mountain fasting and receiving God's Word.[10] Perhaps we need 40 days in His presence, in His Word. If we want more of Him, we need consistent fellowship. Not hitting church on Sunday to get our "Jesus fix" for the week. Not praying only when we need something. Not flipping open the Bible every once in a while. He wants our firstfruits, not our leftovers. We grow in our intimacy by regularly spending time talking to God, worshiping Him, reading His Word, and hiding it in our hearts through memorization.

We are all at different places in our Christian walks. To grow spiritually we must continue to stretch a little more. Maybe you have never established a daily pattern of prayer and time in God's Word. For you, a short prayer and reading a devotional for 40 days may be a big step. Perhaps you are a dedicated prayer warrior who has a solid Bible study routine. Even you may find there is room to go deeper. I was already fairly consistent in praying every morning. I had Bible time with my son on weekdays and often multitasked by reading a chapter or two on my own during breakfast or commercial breaks. For me, more of Him meant quiet time, intentionally set aside to just sit in God's presence with His Word. It also meant committing more Scripture to memory. I added these commitments to my 40 days of self-denial. I believe if we spend time in prayer asking, each of us will find a way we can take one step closer in our relationship, in our level of intimacy with God. A way to get more of Him.

No matter where you are in your walk, being persistent in prayer and immersed in God's Word are instrumental to every step as we continue our *Make Me a Blessing* journey. Prayer and Scripture are the foundation that every blessing package is built upon.

My heart is willing, but my mind needs visual reminders. There's now a picture above my desk in a hand-carved, white-washed frame. "He must increase, but I must decrease." A note on the bathroom mirror. "He must become greater; I must become less." A type-written pendant around my neck. "MORE HE. less me."

Even if our hearts are in the right place, our motives are pure, we have the right attitude, and we don't have any expectations, there are two more To Don'ts we should keep in mind. Don't take on someone else's assignment, and Don't give up.

Don't Take on Someone Else's Assignment

Taking on an assignment that is not our own can prevent us from fulfilling our purpose in blessing. That is why it is so important for us to be empty of ourselves and full of the Holy Spirit. He gives us wisdom, guidance, and discernment to choose our own assignments, those blessings God has planned in advance for us to do. If we do not listen closely for God's direction, we will wear ourselves out trying to be everything to everyone. In doing so, we may miss the specific something He has called us to be to a specific someone.

I can't predict your assignment in blessing, but I will share ideas and examples that I hope will inspire you. Every person has a unique gifting and calling; God will use each of us to bless in different ways right where we are. There are three ways you can apply the illustrations shared in the chapters to come. Adopt. Adapt. Adlib.

ADOPT: Take the example in the book, and use it as is.
ADAPT: Change up the example, and make it your own.
ADLIB: Start from scratch, and come up with an original.

In a mailbox typically filled with bills and advertisements, it is a rare gem to get a personal piece of mail. My husband's stepmother, Pearl, has a gift for correspondence. Since meeting Pearl, I have never had an occasion go unnoticed. In fact, many years I had forgotten my own wedding anniversary until October 16, when I pulled the mailbox open to see a brightly colored envelope with my in-laws' return address label in the corner. Never an ordinary card, Pearl chooses one with the perfect, personalized sentiment. She adds stickers, quotes, verses, and heartfelt words of her own.

I had been so blessed by Pearl's thoughtfulness over the years, I declared I would follow in her footsteps. I decided to **ADOPT** her example by attempting to send a card for every occasion. I lined up birthday, anniversary, and holiday cards for each of my loved ones. I sent out a "Thank you" note for every kindness. It was fun at first, but before long, I was overwhelmed. I beat myself up for giving verbal rather than hand-written thanks. I was stricken with guilt over celebrations not acknowledged with a card. Sending correspondence became another "To Do" on my already never-ending list. Good intentions turned into a pile of unmet expectations. Sincere words were replaced with trite repetitions. My joy was replaced with frustration.

I should not have tried to take on Pearl's assignment. She is truly gifted in that area. Although I can learn from her example, I am not her. God designed us each with our own unique interests and abilities. No one better or more important than another, just different. I did not want to give up correspondence altogether. Instead, I chose to **ADAPT** Pearl's example. I found a happy-medium more suited to my personality and schedule. Rather than sending a card for every occasion, I now occasionally send a card. When I do it's from the heart and meaningful. It doesn't seem rehearsed or forced. Sending notes is a delight because it is no longer an expectation, it comes from a desire to be a blessing.

Maybe neither ADOPT nor ADAPT fits you. Perhaps you feel cards are a waste of money and natural resources; maybe you are in the camp that paper is dead. In any case, you can **ADLIB.** Come up with your own original idea. Being intentional about sending personal emails, texts, or PM's are just a few ways you can acknowledge the people in your life.

Don't Give Up

I commissioned a hand-crafted piece of artwork to remind me of my mission, "Make Me a Blessing." I had a vision for what this would look like, and described it in detail to the artist, including a few pictures from Pinterest. When I picked up the piece, it was not at all what I had in mind. I have to be honest; I was the slightest bit disappointed at first. I thought it would be bigger, brighter. I wanted an attention-grabbing reminder, but it just kind of blends into the room if I'm not looking for it.

Blessing doesn't always look the way we imagined. It may be smaller, less glamorous than we thought it would be. Blessing is hard work that sometimes goes unappreciated. We may end up feeling unnoticed, like we just blend in.

Galatians 6:9 says, "Let us not become weary in doing good, for at the proper time we will reap a harvest if we do not give up."

Don't be discouraged. God sees your effort. He sees your sacrifice even when others don't see it. He will fill you up. He will supply your every need. He will refresh you if you keep pressing on.

The artwork is starting to grow on me. It's not what I expected, but it is a beautiful reminder of the call to bless. Don't lose heart. Don't give up. Blessing is not always easy, but it is always worth it!

CHAPTER 3

Pray
Ask God to Meet Needs

♪Make me a blessing, O Savior I pray,

Make me a blessing to someone today. ¹♪

I have been praying for you, my friend. All throughout the process of learning and writing *Make Me a Blessing*, you, dear sister, have been on my heart. I wish I was there with you now, to clasp your hands in mine. Please allow me to pray over you as we continue to learn and grow together.

Father God, please bless my friend. You promise in Your Word—You will bless her so that she will be a blessing. Make the woman reading these words keenly aware of Your abundant blessing, and inspire her to bless abundantly in return. Open her eyes to see Your face in the faces of others, and may she be compelled to give grace as you have so generously lavished grace on her. Please give this dear sister the wisdom to choose the assignments You have established in advance for her to do. Prepare her heart, equip her for the opportunities You will send her way. Thank You for her willingness to participate in Your Blessing Cycle. Please Lord, complete the cycle by blessing Your sweet daughter in return. In Jesus' name, amen.

There is no greater honor than to have one on One conversation with the Creator of the Universe. Through relationship with Jesus, we are afforded the privilege of speaking directly to God the Father. There is nothing more beautiful, more dynamic than prayer. Communication with God through prayer is the foundation of the Christian life; it is the foundation of being made a blessing.

Going forward, throughout this book, I share some of my own prayers. Examples of how to pray to be made a blessing—Plead and Concede, and how to bless others through prayer—Intercede and Agree. Understand, this is not a suggestion to make doctrine of praying what I pray. There is nothing magical or supernatural about my words. This is simply a representation of what prayer of blessing may look like applied. Feel free to ADOPT—repeat my prayers as is; ADAPT—use the prayers as a guideline; ADLIB—create your own unique blessing prayers.

Plead

On my date night with Jesus those years ago, the concept of blessing shifted in my soul. *Make Me a Blessing* transformed from merely a hymn to the mission of my life— the cry of my heart. Every day, throughout the day, I began to pray those four words. "Make me a blessing." I never could have imagined the impact this petition would have on my life. I challenge you to start praying this simple prayer too. "Make me a blessing." Our Father wants us to ask Him. He longs to put us to work in His Blessing Cycle, but God won't draft us into service; we must enlist. He gave us free will, after all. So throw your hand in the air and shout, "Pick me, Daddy, pick me! I want to be used by You! Make me a blessing!"

"This is the confidence we have in approaching God: that if we ask anything according to his will, he hears us. And if we know that he hears us—whatever we ask—we know that we have what we asked of him," 1 John 5:14-15. We are certain to pray the will of God when we pray the properly applied Word of God. We know it is His will to make us a blessing because we know His Genesis 12:2 promise, "You will be a blessing." He will no doubt grant the requests of His child who willingly asks to be used by Him. Many days I laugh, "I prayed 'Make me a blessing,' and sure enough He did!" Blessing will sneak up and surprise you. Thank God when you recognize His answer to your prayer to be made a blessing.

Self-determination reduces blessing to a check in the box, a good deed for the day. Burn-out is inevitable when we limit blessing to our own ideas, our own resources, and our own strength. "Trust God from the bottom of your heart; don't try to figure out everything on your own. Listen for God's voice in everything you do, everywhere you go; he's the one who will keep you on track," Proverbs 3:5-6 (MSG). Invite God in. Ask Him to lead the blessing. He promises to show the way.

Holy Spirit guidance is the only guarantee we will take on our own assignments. James 1:5 says, "If any of you lacks wisdom, you should ask God, who gives generously to all without finding fault, and it will be given to you." Failure to seek wisdom has caused me to over-commit and under-deliver in blessing. Every misstep is a reminder to back up and pray before I jump in. We were not created to be everything to everyone. As we plead with our Father to use us and guide us, He will indeed show us the exact things He wants us to do. Prayer is the cornerstone of blessing. As we unwrap the other blessing packages, we will continually return to the foundation of prayer.

Concede

When I first started praying, "Make me a blessing," I did not yet realize my-*self* would be an obstacle. I prayed to be a blessing, then reacted poorly when the chance was difficult or inconvenient. I rejected the very blessing opportunities I had asked for because I did not make room in my heart or in my day. Paul said, "For I do not do the good I want to do, but the evil I do not want to do—this I keep on doing," Romans 7:19. That about sums it up for me too.

Blessing won't always fit neatly into our schedules. In fact, God often intentionally interrupts our plans to teach us obedience. This blessing journey does not promise to be convenient. God directs us to bless at times when we don't feel like it, when we'd rather be left alone, when we think we have better things to do. He takes us outside our comfort zones and unsettles our lives.

"For we are God's handiwork, created in Christ Jesus to do good works, which God prepared in advance for us to do," Ephesians 2:10. God planned my blessing walk ahead of time. He created me with the plan in mind. Why then do I insist on trying my own plan first? Why is it difficult for me to surrender when I have a 42-year proven track record of coming up with plans that are shoddy at best? It seems silly when I say it out loud. "As the heavens are higher than the earth, so are my ways higher than your ways and my thoughts than your thoughts," Isaiah 55:9. I need to get over my-*self.* Of course, God's ways are higher; obviously, His plans are better.

A prayer of concession is submitting to God's plans for our days and our lives rather than choosing our own preconceived ideas. In Luke 9, Jesus told his followers to "take up their cross daily and follow me." Though it is a good start, we won't be done after 40 days of beating down our flesh. No, like Paul said in 1 Corinthians 15:31 (ESV), "I die every day!" We must continually surrender our will and relinquish control. Hold nothing back—our time, our treasure, our talent. We concede. We will no longer whine, "Mine!" like spoiled toddlers white-knuckling all the toys. It's all His anyway, to do with whatever He sees fit. This goes hand-in-hand with counting our blessings. Because we are so grateful for what He has given, we are loosening our grip, releasing our control, and handing it all back to Him.

Lord, I concede. All that I am and all that I have is a gift from You and belongs to You. I am handing it back over to You right now. I lay down my plans for today; lead me in Your plan. Open my eyes to see the blessing opportunities you planned in advance for me to do. Thank You, God, for Your unmerited blessing.

We do each have our own personal needs. Scripture abounds with encouragement to bring our requests to God. Big or small, what matters to you, matters to Him, and He wants you to talk to Him about it. Our time together is short; digging into praying for our own concerns would be off-trail. Please understand, I am not saying don't pray for yourself, but it is easy to become so consumed with bringing the long list of our own needs to God, that we fail to pray for anyone else. What we need in this area—oh, honestly, in every area—is balance. God wants us to bring our every concern to Him. When we become others-focused, pleading to be made a blessing, the needs of the people around us will also be our concern.

Intercede

Finally, we have reached the part of the story where we talk about the act of blessing. We are counting our blessings and understanding what the Blessing Cycle means—we are blessed to bless. We have been beating down our flesh and turning away from self-focus by crying out, "MORE HE. less me." We are throwing our hands in the air pleading to be used, conceding our will, and relinquishing our plans. If you're like me, you feel these opening ceremonies have gone on long enough. We want to take off running. We are people of action. Adrenaline is surging; we want to *do* something to be a blessing. This is one reason we may struggle with prayer. It is easy to believe being still means doing nothing. We may even buy into the lie of the enemy that prayer is passive. Prayer often gets reduced to a back-up plan. It's our last resort, after all other efforts have been exhausted. "Hope is gone, all we can do now is pray." The power of prayer gets lumped in with wishing wells and shooting stars. Worse yet, prayer is minimized to the triteness of warm thoughts and best wishes by spouting, "You're in my prayers," without following through. Like it's the thought that counts.

Prayer is the act of asking the only One who can do anything. God accomplished more in four words than any of us will ever achieve with our entire lives. He said, "Let there be light," and there was light. My closest talent is changing a light bulb. God created the intricacy of a human being from the dust of the earth. I can't even build a decent sand castle. Greater than all my scheming and planning, jumping in and doing, it is far more productive to implore the Creator to act on behalf of His creation.

The devil knows the potency of prayer and will try at great lengths to distract us from what is ultimately our most formidable weapon. Prayer is not the equivalent of fingers crossed or sending good feelings out into the universe. Prayer is not passive; it is warfare. James 5:16b says, "The prayer of a righteous person is powerful and effective." If we truly believed this, our prayer lives would never be the same. Prayer would be the first response, not a last resort. We would know prayer is our best defense, not a back-up plan. Prayer would become our main priority, not a minor ritual. If we fully understood the power of prayer, we would not let anything stand in the way. We would drop everything to pray.

PRAY. ENCOURAGE. GIVE. SERVE. SHARE. INSPIRE.

When the problem seems too big—hunger, addiction, terrorism, homelessness—we already agreed not to keep scrolling. But really, what can we do? We can stop looking to ourselves for answers. As children of God, we have the authority to come before His throne and ask Him to step in.

"Arise, LORD! Lift up your hand, O God. Do not forget the helpless. Defend the fatherless and oppressed." [2] Lord, this problem seems too big, beyond human help; please do a work in this situation, as only You can.

Prayer is the universal blessing; its reach is limitless. Unlike our hand-me-down clothes or an offer to help with housework, every single person on the planet, people we may not ever meet, can be touched through our prayers. When you find yourself wishing you could help an estranged loved one, put your wishbone away, and get down on your knees. Even when our offerings are rejected, as we "shrug our shoulders and move on," blessing can be poured out through intercession. Is it wrong that I smirk a little when I pray for people whether they like it or not? "Ha! I prayed for you! What do you think about that?" After their second debate, Ken Ham asked Bill Nye if he could pray for him. Bill Nye replied, "I can't stop you." [3] That's the most accurate thing I ever heard Bill Nye say. No one can keep you from praying for them. Prayer. Is. Unstoppable.

The opportunity to bless through prayer is always available to us. When you are sick in bed wondering how you could possibly bless anyone, pray. In the middle of the night when you can't call to check in, pray. Prayer is not dependent on circumstances, health, or finances. When you are stuck in a blizzard or a hurricane or (insert your region's inclement weather condition here), pray. What's the old postal service slogan? "Neither snow nor rain nor heat nor gloom of night stays these couriers from the swift completion of their appointed rounds." [4] That goes for us too. Our prayers can't be held up from swift delivery. Anytime. Anyplace.

Colossians 4:2a says, "Devote yourselves to prayer." That's not just tossing a few names in with the laundry list. Devotion is applying ourselves completely. In fact, Paul gave the colossal command to pray continually (1 Thessalonians 5:17). Good news, we will never be at a loss for material. There is always, always, always something to be praying. But, truth be told, there are not enough hours in the day to pray for every single need. If you turn on the news for half an hour, you will find enough going on in the world to keep you in your prayer closet until Jesus returns. We must seek wisdom to choose our own assignments even in prayer. Let the Spirit lead, or we will be overwhelmed. Jesus' disciples asked, "Lord, teach us to pray."[5] We need that too.

Our conversations with our Father will vary in length and content. Leisurely talks enjoying His company, passionate cries from the depths our hearts, silent times listening intentionally, blanket prayers to cover multiple needs, quick calls for help. Know that Jesus encourages us to keep it simple. "And when you go pray, do not keep on babbling like pagans, for they think they will be heard because of their many words," Matthew 6:7. God is not impressed by the duration or delivery of our prayers; He looks at the direction of our hearts.

If you need cues on what to pray, the Bible is chock full of ideas. Jesus set the example by praying for the twelve closest in His circle of influence (John 17:6-19). He prayed for their protection and sanctification. We know we are praying God's will when we are praying God's Word with proper application. Pray the prayers in Scripture. Pray the promises in Scripture.

God planned in advance to use you within your circle of influence—your home is the epicenter. Intercession begins in our own homes. Our greatest responsibility is to our own people. Our families need to be covered in prayer. If we don't do it, who will? If we don't make the time to lift up flesh of our flesh, why would anyone else? Your family's every concern, your every concern for them, bring it all to God.

Blessing my family through intercession may not be as easy as it sounds. My prayers are often self-focused, asking God to bend my brood to my will, rather than praying His will be done. When I'm tempted to pray, "Don't let my husband waste money on stupid tools." Instead, I could honor my husband and God by praying, "Help my husband to make wise decisions with the money You've entrusted to us." God's plan is better than my plan for my family; He does not need my suggestions.

Father God, please bless my family. Give my husband the wisdom to lead our household in a manner pleasing to You. Keep him safe as he travels. Give him favor with his employer; cause him to prosper in the work You have given him. Bring him fulfillment and a sense of accomplishment. Keep him in good health. Draw his heart near to You.

I lift my son up to You, Lord. Reveal to him the good plan You have for his life, and give him discernment to follow it. Help us raise him up in the way He should go. Grow him spiritually, academically, in character, and in good health. Develop him to be the man of God You have designed him to be.

Vandalism, suspected drug dealing, things started coming up missing in our neighborhood. Swept up in speculation and worry, I prayed more fervently for God's protection on my family, our home, and our possessions. During morning Bible time, my son prayed his usual list, then added, "God, those people need help. Please get them the help they need." My head hung where moments earlier it bowed. Thanking my son for setting the right example, I confessed to him and to God. My prayers reflected concern for the safety of my family and the security of our things. Self-focus kept me from even considering praying for the people who were, themselves, in spiritual need. Oh, what I often learn from the faith of my child!

Jesus tells us to "pray *for* those who mistreat you,"[6] (*emphasis mine*). I tend to put my own spin on these words by praying *about* a person rather than *for* them. There is a distinct difference. Praying *about* someone brings up their wrongs; praying *for* someone lifts up their needs. Praying about others is selfish, considering only how I am affected; praying for another is asking God to reach into their situation and minister to them. Remember, the Lord doesn't look at outward things that people look at. He looks at the heart. I sometimes neglect to consider what brokenness may cause a person to act out. Every issue has a root cause. Looking merely on the surface never gets to the heart of the matter, the heart of the person.

I huffed when the invitation popped up in my notifications—my friend had started a Facebook prayer request group. "Great! Like I have time for this." That response was not one of my proudest moments. No, I can't pray for every single person, every single day. But let's face it, if I had time to open Facebook, I had some time to kill. My spare time would be far better used seeing who I can bless through prayer, than rolling my eyes at political rants. I have often commented on a Facebook post, "Praying," and continued skimming through memes and selfies without ever pausing to intercede for that need. It may sound obvious, but I had to learn to follow through when I offer to pray. Prayer can be a one-time commitment to a single, simple prayer. Stop for just a moment and pray. Certainly, prayer is far more effective than a comment.

Pray and tell. In many of his letters, Paul told the recipients that he was praying for them and specifically what he was praying for them. If God has laid someone on your heart, and you are praying for their needs, tell them. Be specific. "Today I prayed Psalm 37:4 over you. That God would give you the desires of your heart as you delight in Him." Unwittingly, you just double-dipped—you blessed that person twice. She was blessed through prayer and encouraged by being told about it. If you don't know what to pray, ask. "You've been on my heart. Is there something specific I can pray?" As I have been practicing this, I'm surprised at how many people are completely caught off guard, and equally uplifted by just the question.

I believe wholeheartedly if we are intent to listen, the Spirit of God residing in us will speak. A random person constantly comes to mind. You awake from a dream of someone you haven't considered in ages. Her name keeps coming up in conversation. The name of a person I had never met, my friend's husband, kept popping into my head, every two or three minutes, while I was gardening. After about the 20th time of pushing his name out of my head, I paused to pray. I prayed for him every time for the next 100 times that hour as his name continued to resound. I decided to "pray and tell." My friend didn't divulge her situation, but because they had been struggling, she was blessed by the Holy Spirit's stirring and my obedience. God doesn't need to use us to bless, but for some reason, He chooses to afford us the awesome privilege of participating in His Blessing Cycle.

We are commissioned to bless people through prayer in our immediate circle of influence and beyond. The Bible even challenges us to pray for people we may not know.

Ministers: We have a real enemy who works tirelessly to prevent anyone who would share God's Word. Those called to full-time service of the gospel are constantly under attack.

Lord God, I come to You on behalf of my pastors and the staff at my home church. Protect them and their families; thwart the attacks of the enemy in their lives. Give them wisdom to speak Your Word with boldness so they may build up the believers and be a light to the lost within our church and in our community.

God, I cry out to You for missionaries, teachers, evangelists, and preachers throughout the world. Open doors for them to share the gospel, and allow them to communicate the message clearly.[7] For the ministries and organizations who reach out to the hopeless and afflicted, Lord, equip them. Abundantly meet their needs and cause the work of their hands to prosper for the glory of Your kingdom.

Authority: 1 Timothy 2:2 tells us to pray "for kings and all those in authority." This command applies to your boss, teacher, the governor, the president. I promise not to wax political, but this command does not come with the prerequisite of agreement with those in authority. In fact, the leaders we disagree with are likely in greater need of prayer. That doesn't make it easy, but it is necessary. Remember too, we should pray *for* them, not *about* them. Pray for their salvation. Pray for wisdom.

During a particularly divisive political season, God laid on my heart to pray for the president, who I had not voted for, every time I saw his name or face. On TV, social media, or in the newspaper. Political rants became a cue to pray, rather than a trigger to complain.

Dear Lord, I call upon Your name for those who lead—in our circle of influence, our communities, our states, our countries, and our world. Cause our leaders to rule with wisdom and integrity. Oh God, that Your will be done.

Believers: "Always keep on praying for all the Lord's people," Ephesians 6:18b. As the world grows increasingly evil, the climate becomes increasingly more difficult for God's people. The enemy cannot snatch believers from the hand of the Father (John 10:29), but he can render them ineffective in blessing. Follow the example Jesus set in John 17:20-23 by praying for all believers.

Father, I appeal to You for all Your precious children, redeemed by the blood of the Lamb. Protect them from the schemes of the enemy. Empower them to be a blessing. Stir hearts to bring glory to You. Give believers across the globe the boldness to stand firm in the faith.

Enemies: The words are written in red letters. "Love your enemies, do good to those who hate you, bless those who curse you, pray for those who mistreat you," Luke 6:27b-28. Jesus never gives arbitrary directives; He leads by example. Moments before taking His last breath, after being mocked and brutally tortured and hung on a cross to die, Jesus prayed for the very people who put Him there. "Father, forgive them, for they do not know what they are doing," Luke 23:34b. I cannot pretend that loving our enemies is easy. But I can testify first hand, that praying for (not about) people who have hurt me has brought me freedom. Praying for God to bless those same people, well, that was gut-wrenching. Although they've never apologized, by praying for them I have experienced breakthrough in forgiveness. Even if our enemies never change, blessing them through prayer will change our own hearts.

Dear Lord, You have been an eye-witness to the pain others have caused. Thank you for setting the example of loving our enemies. This is not easy, but I pray You would bless those people who have wronged me. Father, draw their hearts near to You.

Lost: Besides shared origin and being made in the image of God, every person on this planet has another thing in common—a sin nature that leaves us in need of a Savior. Eternity is at stake for countless people who have yet to make Jesus the Lord of their lives.

Dear God, send Your Holy Spirit to sweep through our cities, our nations, and our world. Draw the hearts of Your creation near to You, convicting them of their sin, convincing them of their need for Jesus. Lord, that they would seek You, and that they would find You.

No doubt, there are people in each of our circles, people we know and love, who need to be saved. I want to encourage you to pray for those individuals by name. One way I pray for my unsaved loved ones is to substitute their names in Ezekiel 36:26.

Give _____ a new heart and put a new spirit in_____;
Remove from _____ their heart of stone and give_____ a
heart of flesh.

Did you notice the acronym on the past few pages? Ministers. Authority. Believers. Enemies. Lost. MABEL. I wondered if you've gotten to know me well enough to look for it yet. I don't mind if you think my methods are a bit corny, or a lot corny. When I flounder in prayer, when my mind starts to wander (which is more often than I care to admit), this trick helps bring me back into focus. If I'm stuck in traffic or sitting in a waiting room with nothing else to do, rather than reach for my phone, I should consider who needs prayer. Without a list, I make short work of drawing a blank. If I think, "Who needs prayer? Mabel Franks," each letter reminds of someone to bless with prayer. Ministers. Authority. Believers. Enemies. Lost. Friends. Relatives. Acquaintances. Neighbors. Kids' Connections. Strangers. I never run out of needs to pray for when I use this reminder.

Prayer is the most effective blessing package, and in fact, all the other blessing packages must be rooted in prayer. Because the nature of prayer is not something humanly tangible, we may never see the result. When we give food, we can see people are fed. This side of heaven, we may never know the true effectiveness of our prayers. For several years now, I have felt impressed to pray every time I see flashing lights and hear sirens. I pray for health for victims, wisdom and safety for emergency workers, peace for family members. It only takes a few moments. I often wonder who those prayers may have reached and how those people were blessed. These prayers may never bring closure; we can't always check in a few weeks later to see how God worked in this situation. Prayers like these bring us far beyond self-focus and make us keenly aware of the intricate web of God's universe.

PRAY. ENCOURAGE. GIVE. SERVE. SHARE. INSPIRE.

I was smack-dab in the middle of an important writing project when I heard the sirens in the distance. I felt the nudge in my spirit to pause and pray, but pushed it away, deciding I would pray when I got to a breaking point. Moments later my phone rang. Surprised because my friend usually sends a text, I answered the call. I rushed out the door, crying out to God as I finally answered that nudge to pray. I kept an eye on the firefighter's children, and we watched from a distance as they battled the hay bale fire on my friend's farm. I thank God that no one was hurt, but there was some loss. It was difficult to look my dear friend in the eye as I apologized for not praying immediately. You see, God placed this urgent prayer assignment on my heart. By the time a siren is heard, an emergency is already in progress. There is no time to wait. A person is already injured; a fire is already blazing. Prayer cannot be put off; the assignment is immediate. I repented to God for quieting the prompting of the Holy Spirit. Oh, dear sister, if we continue to silence Him, we will eventually stop hearing His voice. I am not telling you this to guilt you into taking on my assignment. Adopt. Adapt. Adlib. God will surely give you an assignment of your own. When He does, be faithful in obedience to the mission He has given you.

Agree

Adhering closely to our holiday tradition, once again, we were running late for a family gathering. To compound our tardiness, I had not yet purchased my contribution to the shared meal. This meant a dreaded detour to the not-even-close-to-being-on-the-way grocery store.

My husband politely expressed an urgency to keep my in-store visit short. His admonishment was not without merit. By no fault of my own, I unsuspectingly enter any given shopping venue, and each time I am sucked into a time warp—a black hole of clearance racks and special deals. There was no time for bargain hunting that day. I dashed through the aisles grabbing groceries like a contestant on a shopping spree game show. As I rounded the third base freezer section and sprinted for the home plate checkout, I was sure the sobbing woman standing in the pharmacy aisle could feel the breeze as I flew by. The entire exchange I'm about to share occurred in just seconds as I darted through the store, but it played out in my soul in slow motion. I heard in my spirit, "Pray with that crying woman." I reasoned that we were in such a hurry, and my husband was oh-so-patiently waiting in the car. "Dear Lord...." I began in my head, "please touch that woman...." "NO!" My heart stopped as God interrupted me mid-sentence. "I said go back there, and pray WITH that woman!" Although I didn't hear an audible voice, His voice was loud enough within my spirit, that it rang through me head to toe. I halted and made a U-turn.

The woman stood, still wind-blown from my recent passing like a scene from *The Flash*. "Can I pray with you?" Through sobs, her head bobbed in a shallow nod. I clutched her soft, ice-cold hands in mine. I don't remember the words I prayed; words are irrelevant. The power of prayer is not in the words spoken but in the One who hears. Whispers and sniffles revealed she was a pastor's wife, struggling with depression, desperate for an over-the-counter solution. Her tears on my shoulder accompanied gratitude that our loving Father sent me to minister at her very moment of need.

Have you ever felt the weight of a moment strike you with sudden, startling impact? "Bam!" This grocery store encounter hit so hard it took a minute for the percussive resonance to wear off. This was no ordinary coincidence; it was a God-ordained incident. Unmistakably, I was in the right place at the right time, not by my own doing, but due to a Blessing Appointed Moment! BAM!

When I returned to the car, my husband had not even noticed the extra time spent in the store. In reality, it only took a few minutes to share the love of Jesus with this hurting woman. God positioned me intentionally, there and then, for the purpose of reaching that one person. I could have kept scrolling, been too busy to accept my assignment. In fact, I tried. I am so glad He would not let me slide with an excuse. This is why we need to be empty of ourselves and full of Him. So when the Spirit speaks, His voice is not drowned out by our own self-absorption.

A promise to pray for someone is a blessing, and when followed through it is effective. But praying in the moment, with another person ensures we will not forget, and something else happens too. Matthew 18:19-20 says, "Again, truly I tell you that if two of you on earth agree about anything they ask for, it will be done for them by my Father in heaven. For where two or three gather in my name, there am I with them."

That wasn't the last time I was led to pray for a total stranger in public. I'm guessing I may have the opportunity again. Each time I get a little bolder, a little less apt to try to weasel out of it. I have to tell you; it's invigorating to realize you are part of God's bigger plan. To see Him orchestrate your movements and the movements of another person to put you both in the same place at the same time for His purpose. There is such joy in participating in the cycle of blessing He has preplanned! I think the joy is multiplied when He takes us outside our comfort zones. Aren't some of the most delightful experiences those things that come with a little risk?

Oh, friend, I wish I could hear your thoughts on my story. Perhaps you read it and said, "Right on, sister! I love praying with total strangers in public." If that's you, I'm about to speak to someone else for a moment, but please, don't skim onto the next section because you don't think this applies to you. I'm saying that because it's what I would do. One thing I have learned in Bible study is: it's not always about me. Even when the lesson does not apply to us, God does not waste a thing. If you do not struggle with something, you may not be able to relate to someone else who does. But if you've read information on the topic, you can be prepared to give encouragement. Lest you think you don't need this, keep in mind, someone else may need to hear it from you later.

Maybe my prayer story scares you a little bit. It might be far enough outside your comfort zone to pray with a friend, and you are certain I have gone completely crazy if I think you're about to start praying with random people out in the open. Please don't avoid the grocery store for fear the Holy Spirit may strike there again. I promise you; I am not trying to pass out assignments—that is not my assignment. If you willingly listen, God will direct you to the good works He planned in advance for you to do. It is okay if you are uncomfortable with the notion of praying in public. In fact, you're not alone, it's normal. Public speaking is one of the most common adult fears; public prayer is no exception, maybe even more daunting.

I was leading a group of friends in prayer when I completely lost my train of thought. Long, awkward silence was followed by "Ummm...." and even longer, more awkward silence. I finally said, "I don't remember. Amen." No one laughed. They thanked me for praying. God didn't mind. He already knew my requests before I asked. He looks at the heart, not the outward things people look at like compelling words. God honors our obedience, not our eloquence.

I'm no Bible scholar, but as far as I can find, there is not a command, "Thou shalt pray out loud in front of other people." If you read the preceding sentence and said, "Whew! I'm off the hook!" Not so fast; hold tight here for just a moment. While I can't find a command for public prayer, the Bible is riddled with commands to fear not. One of my favorites is Isaiah 54:4a, "Do not be afraid; you will not be put to shame. Do not fear disgrace; you will not be humiliated." Do not allow fear to hold you back from blessing through prayer of agreement. You can overcome the fear of "performing" for your prayer audience and focus solely on the One you are having a conversation with. Though it may not seem like it, talking to God is the same whether someone else is listening or not. Just like any other uncomfortable task, if we practice, we get more comfortable.

I don't like to pray in front of other people.

I'm not good at praying.

I'm too embarrassed.

I hope you can hear my heart as I attempt to speak the truth in love. Maybe you have a good reason that I missed, but the list above is completely self-focused. "How do I feel? How am I affected?" Just for a moment, let's look at how someone else could be blessed if we step out in the area of corporate prayer.

If we always rely on someone else to pray, if the same person is always the one offering prayer, they are never the one who is lifted up in prayer. As words of faith are prayed over your friend, her confidence is bolstered. Knowing the prayer of a righteous person is powerful and effective, the one who hears her need addressed has expectation she will receive an answer.

You may think, "But, I don't know what to say." Your concern is valid. Moses said the same thing to God thousands of years ago in Exodus 4:10. "I have never been eloquent... I am slow of speech and tongue." In the next verse, God reassured him, "Who gave human beings their mouths? I will help you to speak and tell you what to say." God often calls us to step out of our comfort zones and uses us in ways we do not have natural ability. That way He gets the glory instead of us. And, oh sweet friend, God does not stop at telling us not to fear. He tells us to come boldly before His throne! (Hebrews 4:16)

Remember the two foundational factors in every blessing package are being persistent in prayer and being immersed in God's Word. Look to the Bible for direction in prayer. Praying God's Word not only helps us to pray His will, but it builds the faith of the one who hears. "So then faith comes by hearing, and hearing by the word of God," Romans 10:17

(NKJV). As your sister hears God's Word proclaimed over her life, she is emboldened to believe those promises are true, and they are intended for her.

Culture of Prayer

After reciting the Pledge of Allegiance, Mrs. Cribbs asked us to remain standing for a moment of silence. She mentioned she would be praying, but we were each free to do whatever we wished. Pray, meditate, daydream, or take a catnap. The only rule was, we must be silent. Mrs. Cribbs created a culture of prayer in her classroom. She invited us to join her in praying by presenting the option without requiring participation.

On my first visit, the chiropractor extended his hand to shake mine. "Before I get started, I like to pray with my patients. Would that be okay with you?" I had never been asked that during an office visit; of course, I agreed. More surprising than his offer to pray, were the words he spoke. "Give me wisdom in treating this patient. If I am not able to help in improving her health, direct her to the right person who can." This medical professional not only created a culture of prayer in his business. His prayer was a bold example of selflessness and others-focus, as he lifted the needs of the patient over the success of his practice.

You have an assignment within your circle—create a culture of prayer.
Gather a group for "See You at the Pole."
Invite your team members to a pre-game prayer huddle.
Organize an event for the National Day of Prayer.
Ask your co-workers to show up early to pray together.
Get creative in your circle, and develop a culture of prayer.

PRAY. ENCOURAGE. GIVE. SERVE. SHARE. INSPIRE.

A good start is creating a pattern of prayer in our own homes. Bedtime prayers, mealtime prayers—find what works for your family to establish prayer as a life practice. Prayer becomes ritual when we say the same 20 words over supper every night; repetition can cause your prayers to lose their meaning. Sincere words from the heart set the example—no matter when we pray, it's a conversation with our Father God.

Most of us can't help but wonder, "In my everyday life, does what I do really have any significance? After all, I wear a hand-written self-stick nametag that reads, 'Hello my name is.... just a Mom.... just a Wife.... just a Factory Worker.' With a Sharpie-markered label like that, what difference can I make?"

Just a Receptionist blankets every client who enters her office.
Just a Cashier petitions provision for shoppers.
Just a Pharmacist lifts up sick ones whose faces grace her window.
Just a Coach covers the future generation in prayer.
Just a Mom moves mountains for other mamas.

God created you for a purpose. He planted you right where you are for such a time as this. His perfect timing and your unique environment will position you to pray for or with exactly the person who needs it, at just the right time. "And I will do whatever you ask in my name, so that the Father may be glorified in the Son," John 14:13.

Your ordinary life will have eternal impact; you will leave a lasting imprint in your own circle of influence, blessing through the power of prayer. Refuse to wear that "Just a...." label a moment longer. Tear it up! Create a new nametag that reaffirms—your prayers are powerful and effective. "Hello. My name is.... A Mountain Movin' Mama.... A Prayer Warrior Wife." "How can I pray for you?"

CHAPTER 4

Encourage
Meet Emotional Needs

♪Out on the highways and byways of life,

Many are weary and sad;

Carry the sunshine where darkness is rife,

Making the sorrowing glad. ♪

She made up her mind to die that day. Standing amongst shelves lined with pills, the only decision left to make was which bottle would end her pain for good. A stranger walked by, squeezed her shoulder and said, "It will get better. I promise." At that moment, she made up her mind to live.

Do not underestimate the power of encouragement. We are learning the value of what seems small; even so, sister, this is no small thing. *Encourage* is to inject courage into the heart of another, to make her brave. Courage is no small thing. Bravery is no small thing. Encouragement is meeting a person's emotional needs. Her need to be known, his need to belong, their need to be understood.

I'll Pass

For most of my life, I believed there was only one good personality type, and it was not mine. The idea was not without reinforcement; I'd been labeled loud, annoying, abrasive. I dreaded the Book Club assignment to take a personality test and share my findings with the group. I was already fully aware of my personality and tried at length to keep it under wraps. The test results were no surprise: "direct, blunt, critical, not considering the feelings of others." I fixated on those words reinforcing my self-loathing. I ignored the positive words, my good qualities: "leader, articulate, quick-witted, problem-solver."

Why am I telling you this? Because the personality test confirms, I get a pass on encouragement. Romans 12:6-8 talks about using our spiritual gifts: "If it is to encourage, then give encouragement." I don't have that gift. Maryann has a knack for speaking the truth in love. Sheri sees the best in people and is quick to tell them. God has given them both unique personalities for encouragement. It's their gifting. I'll leave touchy-feely to them and keep jumping to action. Right? Nope.

Spoiler Alert: None of us get a pass on any of the blessing packages. There was no pass in *Pray*, and there will be no pass in the next four chapters. Encouragement is no different. Our unique personalities, giftings, and callings will affect how we execute the commands to bless, but they do not exempt us from obedience. Using Romans 12 as an argument, only those who are gifted would be expected to give and serve. We know that's not accurate. 1 Thessalonians 5:11 says, "Therefore encourage one another and build each other up, just as in fact you are doing." Paul is talking to all believers with no gifting prerequisite.

"I'm not comfortable one-on-one. I don't have the gift of encouragement. I lack compassion." For years, I allowed these self-focused excuses to keep me from blessing through encouragement. Maybe your personality differs from mine; you may even have the gift of encouragement. Adopt. Adapt. Adlib. We all have weaknesses. Maybe one of the other five blessing packages is something that doesn't come naturally to you. If we don't get a pass, how do we bless others in ways that don't come naturally, in areas where we are not gifted? The challenge of being uniquely unqualified simply means we have to rely all the more on God's grace. Let's stand on these truths:

I am not who a personality test says I am; I am who God says I am.

I am not limited by my limitations; I can do all things through Christ. [1]

My contribution is not insignificant; His grace is sufficient. [2]

My weakness is not something to hide; I boast that Christ's perfect power rests on me. [2]

"So, as those who have been chosen of God, holy and beloved, put on a heart of compassion, kindness, humility, gentleness and patience," Colossians 3:12 (NASB). Paul tells us to Put. It. On. We don't have to *be* these things; we can choose to *do* them. Don't fake it 'til you make it; be intentional until it becomes instinctual. We can walk in blessings that don't come naturally. God will help us grow until they become part of what we do.

"You have been such an encouragement to me." I looked behind me to see who Maggie was talking to. I was shocked to find there was no one else around. Turns out she was talking to me. Her compliment was an unexpected blessing. Encouragement is not my gift, but God has been so patiently teaching me how to bless by meeting emotional needs. As I hear kind words like Maggie's more and more frequently, I'm less astonished. Still, every time, I remember—that's not me. That is not my personality; it is evidence of Christ working in me because it does not come naturally! "For I know that good itself does not dwell in me, that is, in my sinful nature," Romans 7:18a. We have what it takes to be a blessing because the Spirit of the Living God resides in us. The joy of being used in the Blessing Cycle is multiplied when we know we could not have possibly done it on our own, when we see God's hand at work in the blessing.

Since I had been growing to be an encouragement, did that mean my personality changed? I took the test a second time, just in case. The thing is, my personality has not changed, just like my eye color hasn't changed. You see, a personality is not inherently good or bad; it's simply the person God created us to be. I learned that personality does not dictate behavior; actions and reactions are choices dictated by character. "Critical" and "not considering the feelings of others" are learned behaviors that may be easy for me to slip into because of how I'm wired, but they are not a personality problem; they are a heart problem. God may not change our personalities, but He will surely redeem them by changing our character.

I didn't want to tell you or the Book Club group about the personality test because I was afraid you may look at me differently, that maybe you wouldn't like me. More than once I deleted those paragraphs from this chapter. But I was convicted not to allow self-concern to keep me from transparency that may be a blessing to you. Yes. Appropriate transparency is encouragement and is indeed a blessing. I hope my openness and effort to be real throughout this book will be a blessing to you. Maybe you can identify with my stories and know you're not alone or learn from my mistakes and do it better the first time.

When Andrea let down her guard and opened up to our small group, I knew it would be my safe place. Being my first home Bible study, with women I had barely gotten to know, I was totally prepared to put on my perfect Christian mask and give all the right answers. Andrea's example gave me freedom to drop the façade in a way I had never before experienced. Week after week as the women in our group were simply real with each other, God knit our hearts together, and each one of us experienced tremendous spiritual growth.

If we pretend to have it all together, others will believe something is wrong with them because they don't. Because, honestly, none of us do. But when we share openly about our struggles, we give others the courage to do the same. Let's not mistake being transparent for airing every detail of our sordid mess or blurting out our life story to every person we meet. Being candid in an appropriate way respects boundaries. Transparency is admitting none of us is perfect, and whether people see it or not, we're all going through something. It tells other people they are not alone. When the Spirit leads and conversation flows in such a way, be open and honest for the glory of God.

Let's explore three ways to encourage:

Express. Engage. Experience.

Express: Encourage with Your Words

My trash can overflowed, the floor was speckled with the tiny scraps as pages were ripped from spiral notebooks and tossed across the room. I cleared my desk, put all the pencils away. Gathered three-ring binders and shoved them on the highest shelf where they'd soon collect dust. Trite! Rubbish! Pedestrian! Unoriginal! I gave up writing.

It wasn't long before the text came. "I read your devotional today; it was just what I needed." I nodded my head, smoothed crumpled paper balls, and slipped a binder from the high shelf. I started again. I wish I could tell you this only happened once, and I was permanently convinced to keep going. A thousand times I quit, and a thousand times it was followed by a word of encouragement. God sent friends and on occasion, strangers to build me up. Countless people, obedient in encouragement, spoke a word or sent a message that gave me the courage to persevere. I am certain you would not be reading my words right now except for the blessing of encouragement.

As dinner was winding down, our women's group leader, Heather, stood to admonished us. A sister in Christ would soon take the platform to share her testimony. Our leader wanted to ensure this woman was encouraged after making herself vulnerable. When someone bares her soul, it is our responsibility to build her up, to let her know she has been a blessing. Heather explained, months earlier when she had given her own testimony, the response was chirping crickets. Not one person spoke a single word in response.

Tears trickled down my cheek there at the table, and I all-out ugly-cried on the drive home. You see, four months before, Heather exposed herself by disclosing her raw, personal story. As she shared, my heart was stirred to encourage her for her transparency, for revealing her heart to other women. But it was only my second week in the group of over 200 ladies I had never met. The exchange was likely to be awkward. Besides, I reasoned that she was far too busy with ministry to be bothered. Surely in a group that large, she was surrounded by supporters and was hearing plenty of encouragement.

"If anyone, then, knows the good they ought to do and doesn't do it, it is sin for them," James 4:17. I sinned against God and against my leader by omitting the encouragement I was prompted give. I repented before my Father and then to Heather, who was so gracious to receive my apology.

We cannot assume our leaders know they are impacting our lives. They need our encouragement. The reason we are told not to grow weary in doing well is because people can so easily become discouraged. When she thinks she isn't making a difference anyway; when he feels like a failure or even a fraud. If our ministers aren't encouraged and built up, they may become discouraged and give up. Ministry is hard work. Those leading in the church body are a prime target for the enemy's attacks. We must fight back with encouragement. Don't assume your pastor knows he preached a great message. Don't assume your Bible study leader knows she is making a difference. Don't assume someone else is telling them. We need to tell them.

"But encourage one another daily, as long as it is called 'Today,' so that none of you may be hardened by sin's deceitfulness," Hebrews 3:13. Our friends, our sisters, our children—everyone within our circle of influence needs a fresh dose of encouragement every day. She is in a constant battle. The enemy fights to tear her down. The world fights to tear her down. Her own negative self-talk fights to tear her down. We must wage the war to build her up.

In Exodus 17, God's people fought a fierce battle against the Amalekites. As long as Moses lifted the rod of God, the Israelite army was winning the battle, but as he became weary and lowered his hands, the Amalekites began to win. When Moses no longer had the strength, Aaron and Hur came alongside him, supported him, and held his arms high. God brought the victory through two men who held up their friend. This is a picture of what you and I are called to do for others.

87

God sends us to hold up our friends when they no longer have the strength, so they can experience victory. Galatians 6:2a says, "Carry each other's burdens." When the load is too heavy for her, pick it up, and help her carry it.

How do we build her up and hold her up? It begins with a return to the foundation—being persistent in prayer and immersed in God's Word. Just like every other blessing package, we will not be effective in encouragement with our own words and in our own strength. We must be empty of ourselves and full of the Spirit.

Lord, please make me a blessing through the practice of encouragement. Give me words to speak life into the lives of others. Allow me to be effective in building up those in my circle of influence, so every person I encounter would see You shining through me.

"She opens her mouth with wisdom, And on her tongue is the law of kindness," Proverbs 31:26 (NKJV). Oh, that Proverbs 31 woman! Always raising the bar! Since I was first introduced to her back in seventh grade Home Skills class, she has had me pressing toward the mark. I can tell you, I certainly fall short, but my race isn't finished. I know I don't always open my mouth with wisdom; I have been guilty of letting whatever pops into my head fly from my lips. And I have been known to treat kindness less like a law and more like a guideline. This is why James admonishes us to be slow to speak.[3] He doesn't mean drag out your words and be a slow talker. He means think about it before you shout it. According to Proverbs 18:21a, "The tongue has the power of life and death." Deuteronomy 30:19 says, "Choose life." The best way to speak life-giving words is to speak words straight from the Bible. I can be sure the words of my mouth will be acceptable in God's sight when I speak His Word to other people, to build them up. There are no more encouraging words than properly applied Scripture. My choicest words pale in comparison.

"The mouth speaks what the heart is full of," Luke 6:45b. There is a direct heart-mouth connection. What your heart is full of is what will stream out of your mouth. The water source you're tapped into will flow from your faucet. If I want my mouth to bless others on-demand with encouragement from God's Word, my heart has to be full of it. Titus 1:9 tells us to, "Encourage others by sound doctrine." We can only speak the truth if we know the truth. This does not occur instantaneously. It takes time and dedication to fill up with God's Word. It develops through consistent study, meditation, memorization, and hearing Bible teaching. Input determines output. We must be immersed in the Word so we have a reserve to pull from when we open our mouths. If we pray before we speak, and we are full of Scripture so it naturally flows from us, our words will be wise; our words will be kind; our words will encourage.

When the problem seems too big, well what can we do? You would be surprised; I was. Check out the website of most any mission or ministry, and you will see ways you can reach out with encouragement—cards, letters, messages—to those serving and the ones being served: homeless, victim, orphan, inmate. We may not single-handedly end an epidemic, but we can make a difference in one life through the blessing of encouragement.

Circle of Influence

I have always enjoyed those puzzles: "What's wrong with this picture?" For a while, I had a job asking, "What's wrong with this process?" When my supervisor said I had the gift of minutia, I'm not sure he meant it as a compliment, but I chose to take it as one. Having an eye for detail is a strength, but even the greatest strength can become a weakness when overused. A critical eye can become a critical heart and overflow into a critical mouth. A problem-solver can quickly become a problem-pointer-outer. I'm reminded of the movie "Bambi." Thumper, his bunny friend, commented on Bambi's unstable legs. His mother quickly corrected, "Thumper, what did your father tell you this morning?" Thumper hung his head and replied. "If you can't say somethin' nice, don't say nothin' at all."[4]

"Finally, brothers and sisters, whatever is true, whatever is noble, whatever is right, whatever is pure, whatever is lovely, whatever is admirable—if anything is excellent or praiseworthy—think about such things," Philippians 4:8. We need to be retrained to start asking, "What's *right* with this picture?" But why don't we take it a step further? Not just think these things but retrain our mouths to speak them. When the girl in front of you in the checkout line has killer shoes. Tell her. When the snack mom at your kid's soccer game bakes the best chocolate chip cookies you've ever eaten. Tell her. Search out the good and speak it! Look for the positive and point it out! Be a searchin' and speakin' positive pointer-outer.

I have to be honest, sometimes it's easier for me to encourage strangers than my own people. Maybe it's because I use up all my words nagging. "Pick up your clothes off the bathroom floor; I told you twice today! Don't leave your muddy shoes in front of the door! Stop freezing bugs in my good mason jars!" By the time I have finished, I'm exhausted. The problems are obvious. I often have to be reminded to look at my family and think, "God's face. Give grace." Because our circle of influence begins in our homes, it is of the utmost importance that we effectively bless our own people with encouragement. Be intentional until it becomes instinctual.

We will dig deep into spiritual mentoring later, but in all aspects, coming alongside someone for their personal development is a blessing. As a parent, teacher, coach, or leader, we have the opportunity to mold another person, and often that includes correction. Kindness and truthfulness are not mutually exclusive. In Ephesians 4:15, Paul reminds us to speak the truth in love. His admonishment assures us it is entirely possible to do both simultaneously. "Blessed is the one whom God corrects," Job 5:17a. We cannot be afraid to address an issue for fear it's not loving. Correction can be blessing if it is handled properly. If we only communicate the positive, those entrusted to us will never improve. But, if we err on the side of negative, we could crush the spirit of the one we are meant to grow. Construct and encourage both mean to build up. Sometimes we leave the constructive out of our criticism. Constructive criticism is correction for the purpose of encouragement, for improvement, to build up and not to tear down.

Remember, we are not responsible for the character of the world at large. Before we confront, we must ensure it's our place to speak, and that it is necessary, not nit-picky. Give grace. Let things go that don't matter. We want to foster progress, not force perfection. Trying to be a positive pointer-outer, I attempt to compliment twice as much as I criticize. A technique I like to call a "compliment sandwich" seamlessly incorporates encouragement and correction. If we wedge corrective criticism between two compliments, a person goes away feeling built up rather than torn down.

When correction is necessary, a "compliment sandwich" starts the conversation with a sincere, relevant, positive statement or compliment. The next step is to address the issue in a to-the-point, precise way; not to drag on with "you always" or "every time." It is also important to stay away from words like "however" or "but." These words negate the compliment and render it obsolete. When I say, "Thank you, but...." the other person hears, "Thank you, but disregard my thanks, because you're about to be criticized." When addressing an issue, we should give reasons why if applicable. The purpose is not just to point out the problem, but to offer a solution. "Correction and instruction are the way to life,"

91

Proverbs 6:23b. Finally, we end the conversation on a positive note with another compliment.

Compliment + Correction + Compliment = Compliment Sandwich

Here's a simple example:

Compliment: "I really appreciate that you did the dishes this morning."

Correction: "Next time, please remember to wipe the spilled water from the floor,"

Reason Why: "so no one slips."

Compliment: "I am so proud of how responsible you are becoming!"

Correction is not counter to encouragement, but it must be tempered with it. Paul set the example of the compliment sandwich in his letter to the Philippians. He opens with a positive. "In all my prayers for all of you, I always pray with joy because of your partnership in the gospel from the first day until now," Philippians 1:4-5. He continues with a correction. "Do nothing out of selfish ambition or vain conceit. Rather, in humility value others above yourselves, not looking to your own interests but each of you to the interests of others," Philippians 2:3-4. He finishes on a good note. "I rejoiced greatly in the Lord that at last you renewed your concern for me," Philippians 4:10a.

Considering Paul's correction, "value others above yourselves," I wonder, how do we convey to others that they are valued? Our Father God, who calls us highly valued, always sets the example for us to follow. He sees us (Genesis 16:13); He smiles on us (Psalm 119:135 (NET)); He calls us by name (Isaiah 43:1). I am moved to tears at the thought. Look people in the eye; let them know they are seen. Smile; let the light of Jesus shine through you. Ask and learn and speak a person's name; it shows respect, meets their need to be known, acknowledges their value.

God conveys our value in more ways than I can express; entire volumes could be written. Before we move on, I want to talk about one more way that is near and dear to my heart. God calls us "friend" (John 15:14-15). Adult relationships aren't nearly as easy as when we were children and could walk up to someone on the playground. "Do you want to be my friend?" As we get older, friendships take time; there's a vetting process; insecurity has us questioning whether the other person even likes us. On our second or third meeting, I walked through the door, and my sweet Jesus-sister Pam cheered, "Hello, friend!" I am suddenly whisked back to fifth grade when my beloved teacher called me friend. I told you, I didn't quite understand the impact of it then, but I do now. We don't get to choose our family or really anyone else in our circle of influence, but we do get to choose our friends. I have decided to ADOPT the example set by God, mirrored by Pam and Mrs. Cribbs, to show people value by calling them "friend." The title friend means you are accepted, you are chosen, you belong to me.

"Rejoice with those who rejoice; mourn with those who mourn," Romans 12:15. Share in their joy; share in their sorrow. Encourage the people in your circle of influence by making what matters to them matter to you. The Message says, "Laugh with your happy friends when they're happy; share tears when they're down."

Celebrate her! Be his biggest fan! Make their win your win! Praise God with them! When Elizabeth gave birth to John the Baptist, her friends and neighbors heard, and shared her joy! (Luke 1:58)

Let what breaks her heart break yours. Make his loss your loss. Cry with them. "When Jesus saw her weeping, and the Jews who had come along with her also weeping, he was deeply moved in spirit and troubled. Jesus wept," John 11:33, 35.

Gratitude

Let's go back to our "Count Your Blessings List." I hope your list has been growing, that you've continued to document how truly blessed you are. Every gift is from God, but He often uses people to deliver them. As you look back over your list, consider who participated in blessing you; make a point to thank them. Gratitude is a direct continuance of the Blessing Cycle as we bless with encouragement those who have blessed us. Don't forget what seems small. When we acknowledge the small things as having blessed us, we will recognize the small things we do as being a blessing.

"Now we ask you, brothers and sisters, to acknowledge those who work hard among you, who care for you in the Lord and admonish you," 1 Thessalonians 5:12. We talked earlier about encouraging our leaders, but let's also remember the others who serve in the church. It only takes a second to roll down the window and shout, "Thanks for serving!" to the guy who directs traffic in the church parking lot. It doesn't take any time to say it as we grab a bulletin or top off our coffee cup with hazelnut creamer. These folks give their time to serve, so the rest of us can concentrate on worship and hearing the Word.

Those who protect and serve our communities and our nation—military, law enforcement, fire and rescue, security—deserve our gratitude. Freedom is not free. Safety and security do not come without cost. "Greater love has no one than this: to lay down one's life for one's friends," John 15:13. Often there are tell-tale signs: a uniform, a bumper sticker, a veteran ball cap. When we spot it, "Thank you for your service," is all it takes to bless with the encouragement of gratitude.

Engage: Encourage with Your Presence

"Practice hospitality," Romans 12:13b. Does the word hospitality make you picture a lady with red lipstick and a bouffant hairdo, wearing high heels and an apron while holding a steaming apple pie in her potholder-gloved hands? "The friendly and generous reception and entertainment of guests, visitors or strangers," may put us in mind of a party hostess. I doubt Paul was recruiting the next Martha Stewart when he gave this instruction. Hospitality begins when we engage people, invite them in, and include them.

"Some of the moms walk together during gym class. Would you like to join us?" Sheri's invitation forever changed my life. Neither of us knew that walk would sprout a Bible study and develop into rich, life-long friendships. From those relationships came the deepest time of spiritual growth I had ever experienced. Her simple act of inclusion had eternal impact.

"Get along with each other; don't be stuck-up. Make friends with nobodies; don't be the great somebody," Romans 12:16 (MSG). Reach out. You don't have to be everyone's best friend; Jesus had an inner circle of close friends, and it is okay if we do too. But we are called to love everyone. Remember the forgotten. Embrace the neglected. Include the excluded. Accept the rejected. Encourage her by meeting her need to belong.

My illness didn't keep me from church that morning, but I purposed to slip in and out unnoticed. I sunk in my seat hoping Tammy wouldn't see me from three rows up where she was sitting at the other end of the aisle. But soon our eyes met and her lips widened to a smile revealing every tooth in her mouth. Clutching her purse in one hand and her Bible in the other, she happy-danced over to the seat next to mine. "Lord, I know I prayed 'Make me a blessing' this morning, but I do not have the energy to be 'on' today." God already knew that little tidbit before I told Him. It turns out, Tammy didn't need me to be "on;" she did all the talking. She just needed someone to listen, which I could do sitting perfectly still without saying a word. In addition to telling us to be slow to speak, James also says in chapter 1 verse 19, "Be quick to listen." Listening is usually difficult for me. I often have to pray and be intentional to not monopolize the conversation. So that day, when I didn't feel up to talking, I was in the perfect position to bless Tammy in the way she needed. Sometimes we don't need words at all to bless with encouragement.

When words fail us, we may be tempted to avoid an awkward situation. A friend's diagnosis leaves us speechless, so we avoid her rather than risk saying the wrong thing. A tragic death paralyzes our sensibilities, so we stay home from the funeral instead of facing the family at their most broken. Self-focus once again keeps us from reaching out for fear we may look stupid. We are far more concerned about feeling uncomfortable than being a comfort. The truth is, we don't always need the right words. Our presence can mean far more than any concocted well wish. Job understood this. He had lost everything—his livestock, his livelihood, and his ten children. In chapter 2 of Job, his friends came "to sympathize with him and comfort him," but they were at a loss for words. "Then they sat on the ground with him for seven days and seven nights. No one said a word to him, because they saw how great his suffering was." Often encouragement isn't about words at all. In fact, later on in Job's story when his friends finally did open their mouths, their words were anything but encouraging. It is okay to say, "I wish I had words, but I don't. I'm here." Sometimes the greatest blessing is to just be.

Our family is restoring an adorable little nearly-off-grid cabin built by Lannie and his son in 1980. Once a week or so, 88-year-old Lannie would stop by, perhaps to visit the cabin just as much as its residents. All the same, to him it was just a friendly visit, but to us, it was so much more. Being driven and goal-oriented, I can be a bit of a taskmaster with my son. In the rush to get things done, I quickly forget little boys need breaks, in the same way, I forget busy mommies need breaks. But when our friend stopped, so did all the work. The timing was rarely coincidental. When Asa shouted, "Mr. Lannie's here!" I knew it was a cue, a wink from my Father. It's time to rest. So that was just what we did. We offered our friend a mug of hot coffee before noon or a frosty glass of lemonade after midday. We sat, and Lannie told grand stories of the good ole days. He had a lifetime of experiencing God's faithfulness. His simple stories were often interwoven with profound insights. His visits offered compliance with God's commands—Rest. Be still. In being a friend, dropping by to visit, Lannie became one of my life's great blessings.

Asa and I cherished our visits to Grandma Phyllis's house. We spent afternoons playing cards or doing crossword puzzles. Looking back, I wish I had taken the time more often to sit, to visit, to listen to the same story for the 100th time. I let a packed schedule be an excuse for the infrequency of our time together. But to be honest, we make time for what matters to us, for what we value most. Sometimes we don't appreciate people until they are gone. Grandma is in heaven with Jesus now. I know she forgives me, and we will be together again soon. I cannot change the time I didn't spend with her, but I can make the most of the time I have with the people who are still here.

You see, we can be a blessing by simply being a part of someone's life, by being present. Just a visit, just checking in, just being a friend can encourage another person.

Experience: Encourage with Your Story

Mary received arguably the greatest honor ever bestowed on a woman. She would give birth to the Messiah! This amazing gift likely did not come without concern on the part of this young girl. A pregnant woman in any century has a monumental list of questions. "Am I eating right? Is the baby growing? Have I overdone it? Is this normal? Should I feel this sick? What is this pain in my side?" My guess is, it was exponentially more difficult in an age without WebMD, Google, and the "What to Expect" books. God in His sovereignty did not leave Mary to fret it out for nine months. He sent her a friend, a mentor, who was two trimesters ahead in pregnancy. Elizabeth didn't just *comprehend* Mary's situation. She *identified* with recency. If you asked me a pregnancy question today, I'd have no clue. In the past 15 years, I have forgotten all the little things. But it was all fresh for Elizabeth. For the first three months, Mary had a friend to hold her hand and guide her through. She left in Elizabeth's ninth month, which meant Mary went away encouraged with an entire pregnancy's worth of Elizabeth's experience.

Cheryl and I made plans to meet at a coffee shop where we could get to know each other and our boys could play chess. It was no coincidence when she told me about her family's out-of-state move. You see, for all 39 years of my life, I had lived within a 50-mile radius in two adjoining counties. But just weeks earlier, we found out we would be moving several hours away to another state. I was determined to trust God. Still, I was a little apprehensive. How would we meet new people? Especially since we homeschooled. What would we do with no family nearby? Cheryl wasn't able to answer all my questions, but her experience encouraged me. Hearing God's faithfulness to her family, reminded me He promises to take care of all my needs too. God is so good to connect us with just the right person to build us up when we need it.

It is a beautiful thing when God allows us to encourage others with our experience, but it does not always come from a place of joy. Sometimes, He brings beauty out of ashes. Often, blessing accompanies a tear-stained handkerchief; encouragement comes in the form of mutual devastation. A diagnosis given. A marriage falling apart. A loss endured. "Praise be to the God and Father of our Lord Jesus Christ, the Father of compassion and the God of all comfort, who comforts us in all our troubles, *so that* we can comfort those in any trouble with the comfort we ourselves receive from God," 2 Corinthians 1:3-4 (*emphasis mine*). I hope you noticed the "so that" in this verse. God's Word continues to be reflective of the Blessing Cycle. Our Father comforts us, not simply for our own good, but also so that we will have comfort to give when others need it. We are blessed so that we can be a blessing; we receive so that we can give; we are comforted so that we can be a comfort. We have to shake off our self-focus, even at our darkest times, and allow our hurt to be transformed.

Well-intentioned people say they "understand" because they *comprehend* a difficult or tragic situation. But there is a distinct comfort that can only come from someone who understands the pain because they *identify*. Someone who has endured the same hardship, experienced the same loss. When another person shares their story and we can see our own struggles, we understand on a whole new level that we are not alone. Sometimes we really need to hear from someone who has been there or is currently right where we are.

I am honored and humbled to introduce you to my dear friend Brenda, a woman who has been instrumental in my spiritual growth. She encourages and inspires me and countless others in the way she has allowed God to use her story to be a blessing. I cannot find adequate words to express what God has done through Brenda's life, so she has graciously agreed to share her story in her own words.

Brenda's Story

After a few months of concern over symptoms we were noticing in our 5-year-old daughter, we were shocked to hear that our Kayla had the worst-case scenario, an inoperable tumor in her brainstem. On Aug 25, 2005, a team of specialists came into her Columbus hospital room and the pediatric neurosurgeon announced the technical name of the tumor. Desperately reaching for hope and reassurance, but trying to not worry Kayla, I simply asked if it'd be okay. The doctor understood my question, but knowing the grave prognosis he quietly replied, "She may not survive." The next moments of my life were utter shock and confusion. Later that evening my husband and I met with the neurosurgeon and learned that her prognosis for survival was 6-9 months.

It's 2 Corinthians 1:3-4 that tells us that we are comforted so that we can comfort others. Well, news spread quickly, and family and friends comforted us with every bit of encouragement and love they had. Even before we left the hospital, Kayla was spoiled with all sorts of gifts. People brought meals during her treatments, Christian friends sent Bible verses that we clung to, friends raised money through several fundraisers, and it was all so very needed and humbling. God connected me to Christian women who understood our journey because they had been there. Early on, I spent hours talking to a sweet mom whose daughter was diagnosed shortly before Kayla. God then connected me to Diane, who had been through her own intense medical emergencies that gave her compassion and understanding of my trial. She came alongside me and guided me spiritually through these often fearful years of my life, spending countless hours e-mailing, talking to me, and showing me how to dig deep into God's word to survive this journey.

God blessed us so greatly, and Kayla survived much longer than expected. When we hit the 4-year mark and she was doing well, we really thought God had healed her. It wasn't long after that we noticed little symptoms returning. When an inoperable tumor returns, there aren't many options. We enacted Plan B and lived in Cincinnati for a month to try some new treatments. When we confirmed the treatments weren't working, we went on hospice care and were allowed to try Plan C as well as to exhaust a few other treatments as to have no regrets. God sent more people who had "been there" into my life. A dear mom tearfully shared with me her daughters end of life because I wanted to know what to expect. God blessed us with Sandy who brought us medical equipment and even brought her son's physical therapist to help us get Kayla comfortable. Sandy had just lost her son months before to the same tumor and was on call for me 24/7 those last months of Kayla's life. Kayla went to her heavenly home on June 18, 2010, at age 10.

I had certainly been loved with a 2 Corinthians 1 type of comfort. We were prayed for by thousands of people and God had provided me ladies who had "been there" to walk along with me, not to mention how our physical needs were met. So how do you use this hard mess to comfort others? I didn't have to look hard to find others to reach out to. God just put them in my path.

During the diagnosis and treatment years, we found thousands of families that had been or were on the same journey, and we got to know some of them well. There were moms that I would talk to on the phone, and we've met many families in person. We still get together with some and even vacation with a few. There is such a deep connection with the families that know exactly what you're dealing with. Because Kayla survived so long, we had an "in" with desperate families looking for survivors. We shared treatments with hundreds of families and continuously pointed them to God as they desperately tried to cling to something to survive this impossible journey. Our CaringBridge website was a handy tool to update people quickly on our progress, share our treatments, and remind ourselves ways that we could see God in this.

As the medical part of this journey gets progressively further behind us, I've realized that my ministry in this is different now. I'm finding because of my experience, I have a confidence to come alongside folks hurting from a variety of hard trials. If you've gone through a hard trial, I pray you also are realizing that you have grown in confidence and see that God has given you credibility and less fear to reach others. Anyone that has gone through a painful trial earns a credibility, one that they never wanted, for people to look at you and say, "you understand," to their situation. People share because they know you've been through difficult stuff. It doesn't matter what the details are, I can still listen and relate because I know God's grace in the hard time. Along with earning credibility because of pain, I've also lost my fear of "what to say." It used to be scary to reach out to people in such pain. I would justify my avoidance of those hard situations by thinking I was helping by not inconveniencing them for a visit or call. But during our hardest times with Kayla, I really realized how much those people need others to connect with and that they are still just human.

I do reach out to people that have lost a child, but I also strive to reach out to anyone God puts in my path that needs someone to talk to. Whether it's that first holiday with an empty chair, a spouse that left, how to answer that excruciating question of "how many kids do you have" after you've lost one, or that 5th anniversary of a loved one's passing, I often feel a nudge to share part of my story about Kayla to help someone know they aren't alone. And when I do share, it's as much of a blessing for me to hear what God has done for them as it is for them to see that only by God's grace have I survived and am stronger than before.

We all have painful times in life and no matter what your hard experience is, please be encouraged to come alongside someone. It's been eight years since Kayla's cancer returned and she passed away and I can still tell you those who visited and called in those last few months. Even if I was too busy to talk long, I knew they cared and put forth bravery in a way not many do. I adore those that visited us at the funeral home to show their support and love. People loved us in many ways and even if they didn't know what to say or the words didn't come out well, we knew they cared and were thankful for their presence.

I'll never be able to love enough to equal how much people loved us, but because of this situation, I can be a more confident blessing to others. With whatever situations you've faced, pray about what kind of ministry you can have to comfort others, help them not feel alone, and pray for them to persevere through their hard time.

I am beyond grateful that Brenda was willing to share her experience to encourage us. Brenda's story is not hers alone; it is Jesus' story. The proof positive of His desire to reach people with His love and how sometimes He allows us to participate.

Your Story

In John 6, Jesus had just five loaves of bread and two fish to feed five thousand men, plus women and children. "When they had all had enough to eat, he said to his disciples, 'Gather the pieces that are left over. Let nothing be wasted.' So they gathered them and filled twelve baskets with pieces of the five barley loaves left over by those who had eaten." God does not waste a thing. He gathers up your broken pieces and gives you back more than you had when you began.

If you are in the middle of a trial, please allow me to encourage you right now with the truth of Romans 8:28. All things will work together for your good. It is a promise to those in Christ. Not everything that happens to us will be good. In fact, in John 16:33b Jesus says, "In this world you will have trouble. But take heart! I have overcome the world." God will bring you through. Abuse. Abandonment. Divorce. Disease. What seems like a waste, what seems like crumbs and scraps, what you may want to hide or even forget. When you have overcome, and sometimes right in the midst of your pain, God will not waste a thing. He will gather up your crumbs, all your broken pieces, and you will have more left over than you had when you started. This is the miracle God will perform with your story. He will turn your mess into your message. He will open doors for you to minister the blessing of encouragement to others through your experience. He will use your story to breathe life into others.

"Hardships often prepare ordinary people for an extraordinary destiny."[5] Joy or pain, you have a story. Allow God to use it to make you a blessing. Like Brenda told us, you won't have to look far for people to reach out to. God will put others in your path for you to bless; He will reveal the target audience in need of encouragement from your unique experience.

"Let the redeemed of the Lord tell their story," Psalm 107:2a.

He will use your happiness to bring hope.

He will allow your celebration to invite expectation.

He will take what nearly broke you and break chains for someone else.

He will use what bound you to set others free.

He will turn your misery into ministry.

Let your story bring God glory.

CHAPTER 5

Give
Meet Material Needs

♪Give as 'twas given to you in your need,

love as the Master loved you; ♪

"**O**ne day at three o'clock in the afternoon, Peter and John were on their way to the Temple for prayer meeting. At the same time there was a man crippled from birth being carried up. Every day he was set down at the Temple gate, the one named Beautiful, to beg from those going into the Temple. When he saw Peter and John about to enter the Temple, he asked for a handout. Peter, with John at his side, looked him straight in the eye and said, 'Look here.' He looked up, expecting to get something from them. Peter said, 'I don't have a nickel to my name, but what I do have, I give you: In the name of Jesus Christ of Nazareth, walk!' He grabbed him by the right hand and pulled him up. In an instant his feet and ankles became firm. He jumped to his feet and walked," Acts 3:1-8 (MSG).

Such as I Have

My silly grin might have been accompanied by a little "woohoo" and the slightest fist pump. In front of each seat lining the round tables was a stack of papers neatly stapled in the top left corner. The bold typed heading danced up to meet my eyes. "Spiritual Gift Quiz." I know that response seems polar opposite of my reaction to the personality test I told you about in the last chapter. I'm kind of a nerd for quizzes and surveys when I don't suspect they have been designed for the sole purpose of shaming me.

My main areas of spiritual gifting were no surprise to me. Most of us know where we thrive and what makes us feel alive. Our passions, what stirs our souls, what energizes us—these are usually good indicators of our God-given purpose. The test affirmed the gift of teaching, and I also scored high in giving. Although giving gets me giddy, at that time in my life, Peter's words could have just as easily escaped my lips. "I don't have a nickel to my name." I laughed at the tallied quiz results in my hand. "That's funny God! How am I supposed to give more than I already am when I'm borrowing from tomorrow just to keep the bills paid?" How could I possibly fulfill my giving gifting with nothing to give? After all, the only way I would have been dropping an extra wad of cash into the offering plate is if I had asked the bank teller to issue my paycheck in one-dollar bills. You see, I mistakenly believed giving was exclusive to the money I drop in the plate at church. Though God's Word is clear on the importance of what is referred to as tithes and offerings, those are, in fact, only a small part of how He allows us to bless through giving. *Give* is meeting material needs; including but not limited to money. It turns out, I had a lot more to give than I originally understood.

Scripture tells us the lame beggar expected to get something from Peter and John. What he received was most certainly beyond his greatest expectation. In the King James

Version of Acts 3:6, Peter said, "Silver and gold have I none; but *such as I have* give I thee: In the name of Jesus Christ of Nazareth rise up and walk," (*emphasis mine*). Peter did not brush off the beggar with the assertion he had no money. What he had to give was far more valuable than money anyway. Our bank balances don't get us a pass on blessing any more than our giftings and personalities do. Each of us has a unique "such as I have" to meet the needs in our own circle of influence. We see in 2 Corinthians 9:10 that God supplies seed to the sower. Our Father has already equipped every one of us to fulfill our calling to give, and He promises to continue equipping us. We have each been blessed materially so that we will bless through giving.

It was a leap of faith when my husband and I decided I would leave a good-paying job in order to homeschool our son. Cash got a little tighter, but as life grew simpler, it also became much richer. Starting what we lovingly refer to as our microfarm had long been a dream. The necessity to off-set my loss of income had finally made our dream a reality. Split-rail fence soon outlined a pasture next to the barn where free-range chickens, dairy goats, and black guinea hogs took up residence. Raised garden beds were planted behind rows of vineyard and orchard.

"Honor the LORD with your wealth, with the firstfruits of all your crops," Proverbs 3:9. For most people, the practical application of this command would be to give a portion of their paycheck earnings. For us, the microfarm was more than a hobby, it was our livelihood, our major food source. Though we gave from my husband's income, I was no longer receiving a paycheck. God stirred me to give from the literal firstfruits of my physical labor—the food harvest from our microfarm. Long before the days of direct deposit, a harvest of grain and livestock would have been the offering the Old Testament people brought to the Temple. "A tithe from everything from the land, whether grain from the soil or fruit from the trees, belongs to the LORD; it is holy to the LORD," Leviticus 27:30. In that season, my harvest became a "such as I have." I didn't have much money to spare, but I had food in abundant supply. As I went about my work tending to the microfarm, I prayed diligently over our animals, over the garden, and over those who would be nourished by the resulting crop. God allowed me to participate in the Blessing Cycle by feeding His people. Green beans and carrots and spinach and ham overflowed from my home into the kitchens of others.

My son amused me and our friend, Mr. Lannie, with the latest variation of his ever-changing future career plans. In the previous week, he had gone from wanting to be an entomologist, to a lawyer, to presently the largest goat farmer in Washington County. "There's not much money in eggs. I don't think I want to have very many chickens," Asa said. "Well, every little bit helps," Lannie chimed in. "When I was younger we did a little here and there. It all adds up." "Well," Asa answered. "I think at a couple of dollars per carton, I'd rather just bless my friends with the extra." Hearing those words from my young man was a proud mama moment. That's what we did, too. We kept a few laying hens, enough to provide eggs for our family. A dozen or so were left over every week to give away. This "such as I have" may seem small. I mean, eggs cost how much? Two bucks? But in fact, I know first-hand what a blessing a carton of eggs can be.

As the sun peaked through the eastward facing windows that Monday morning, I started a batch of broth simmering in the crockpot. That evening we would have one of our favorites, homemade chicken and noodles. When possible, I tried to make it all from scratch, so half an hour before dinnertime, I began gathering noodle ingredients. I retrieved the mat and rolling pin from above the stove, stepped into the pantry to grab the flour canister from the top rack, and snatched the salt carton on my way out. I swung open the refrigerator door to reach for the eggs, and my heart sank as my hand met the empty glass shelf. There were no eggs; we were completely out. That meal was our only option. The cupboards were bare besides staples. The roast in the freezer would take hours just to thaw, not to mention several more to cook. I leaned against the cold tile of the kitchen counter, when across the room the cardboard carton on the farmhouse table caught my eye. You see, Brenda showed up for Bible study earlier that afternoon, bringing with her a dozen farm-fresh eggs. My hens had not yet begun to lay, and store-bought eggs cannot compare, so I was sincerely grateful for the gift. But while prepping dinner, I realized, Brenda's eggs were more than just a welcome treat; this was another Blessing Appointed Moment! BAM! Brenda's eggs had saved dinner! And so much more than that, God's promise for provision was reinforced in the gift. There are no small blessings. You may never know the huge impact of your seemingly small contribution.

Different seasons in life bring a different "such as I have." At one time, I had mastered the art of couponing. In that way, my financial contribution was saving money on the grocery budget. Items scored for free or cheap quickly became more than just the three of us could use. In the spirit of giving firstfruits, I placed a basket in the kitchen to tithe from shopping trips. Each week as groceries were put away, a few items would be set aside to donate to the church food pantry. Shampoo, toothpaste, and mouthwash often cost little or nothing, but were my "such as I have." God had amply blessed me to make me a blessing in return.

We know it by heart now. We are blessed so that we can be a blessing. Not so that we can build a bank. "Do not store up for yourselves treasures on earth, where moths and vermin destroy, and where thieves break in and steal. But store up for yourselves treasures in heaven, where moths and vermin do not destroy, and where thieves do not break in and steal. For where your treasure is, there your heart will be also," Matthew 6:19-21. Now, I did not go overboard to become a crazy-

111

couponer-turned-hoarder. You know, spare rooms and basements and outbuildings crammed full; one person has more in their stockpile than could be used in three lifetimes. What is reality for a few, can be a metaphor to inform others of us squirreling away our own more-than-plenty. When I asked God to reveal my "such as I have," he began dealing with my heart about my own version of hoarding. Not as seen on TV, but in neatly stacked totes and boxes, I tidily stored far too many unused things, just in case they may be needed someday. Unopened craft supplies from ten years previous. Toys, books, and games my son had long ago outgrown. Luke 3:11 says, "Anyone who has two shirts should share with the one who has none, and anyone who has food should do the same." While having a second shirt doesn't seem like a surplus, the Bible tells us it is if our brother or sister has none. So certainly, those six totes of clothes I hadn't worn in 50 pounds could have been a blessing to someone else.

God supplies us with extra to give to those in need. He always gives us just enough. Not too much or too little. What is over and above, beyond our needs, isn't to pocket; it's to pass on. "At the present time your plenty will supply what they need, so that in turn their plenty will supply what you need. The goal is equality, as it is written: 'The one who gathered much did not have too much, and the one who gathered little did not have too little,'" 2 Corinthians 8:14-15.

The truth is, my storing up of material goods with the remote possibility they would come in handy one day down the road was an indication of a heart issue. The real reason I was holding on to things and holding back in blessing was a poverty mindset. I did not trust God to supply my future needs. What we have in surplus right now is for the purpose of giving. Don't worry about tomorrow. "And my God will meet all your needs according to the riches of his glory in Christ Jesus," Philippians 4:19. We can trust Him to keep His promises. But, there is a tendency to quote Scripture without considering context. Paul acknowledged the Philippians' generosity in meeting his needs. "You sent me aid more than once when I was in need," Philippians 4:16b. He said, "God will meet all your needs," in the context of the Philippians having met Paul's needs. He is explaining the Blessing Cycle! You see, the promise of supplied needs is precluded by the act of supplying needs.

So, what is your "such as I have"?

If you need help getting started, go back to your growing Count Your Blessings List. "Each of you must bring a gift in proportion to the way the LORD your God has blessed you," Deuteronomy 16:17. As we remember how we have been blessed, I am certain we will find to be true what my friend Mary says, "God not only supplies all of our needs but also some of our wants." Spend time in prayer asking God to identify the surplus He has given you so that you will be a blessing.

Many of us do live paycheck to paycheck and struggle to stick to a tight budget. We consider ourselves poor because our cars are 10 years old, we haven't had new clothes since two Christmases ago, and our families only go on vacation when someone dies or gets married. I don't know your situation, but I would guess most of our lives do not remotely resemble what poverty really looks like. Some months in my 20's were spent dining on hotdogs and ramen noodles, but I have never missed a meal due to want. On occasion, my closet has been full of last year's styles that don't fit quite right, but I have never gone without adequate clothing. For a season, my budget restricted me to generic shampoo, but I have never lacked straight-from-the-tap, fresh water for drinking and bathing. My mattress has seen better days, but I have never been deprived of a safe place to sleep at night. Countless millions of people around the world cannot make those same statements.

Diez y Ocho de Octubre

The next stop on our high school mission trip would be a small village in Monterrey, Mexico. Named for the day it was founded—Diez y Ocho de Octubre is Spanish for October 18. Our host church had arranged an outdoor service where we would pass out the Bibles we had smuggled across the border. One of our new friends, Aurora, escorted us door-to-door as we invited villagers to join the service. Door-to-door is an overstatement. Each shack was a patchwork of random, found materials pieced together. Even the nicest of the barely-standing, dirt-floor houses had no more than a soiled, tattered sheet hanging in the doorway. The truth is, in America, our pets would be taken away if we had them living in the conditions these families called home.

I made sport of kicking a rock back and forth as we traveled down the dusty path. A firm tug on my shirt tail was accompanied by melodic words I could not understand. My eyes met deepest pools of black fixed beneath a matching head of stringy hair. I replied, "Repita por favor." I knew enough to ask the bony framed girl to repeat what she had said, but after three years of Spanish classes, I could not make out a word she uttered. "Repita por favor." I don't know why I continued asking. Her repeating would not change my lack of understanding. Aurora, giggled, stepping in to translate. "Be careful of your shoes, you will ruin them." I had picked up the cheap pair of white canvas tennis shoes just before the trip. "They were only three bucks; I'm going to throw them away when I get home anyway." Before those words that had quickly formed in my mind could shamefully exit my mouth, I caught a glimpse of tiny brown feet covered in grey dirt, toenails jagged, soles protected by nothing but callouses.

I testified before audiences at school, at church, and at youth group of how my experience at Diez y Ocho de Octubre had forever changed my life. The little barefoot girl brought to light my carelessness and ingratitude. At that moment when

I came face-to-face with real need, I vowed to never again take for granted all I had been given. I would always remember the faces of poverty. Fast forward twenty years, and there I was, laughing at a Spiritual Gifts Quiz, having long forgotten, insulting God by saying His blessing wasn't enough for me to share. Sadly, if you came to my house today, you'd find more pairs of shoes owned by just the three of us than were possessed by the collective residents in the entire village of Diez y Ocho de Octubre.

When we have seen real poverty first hand, after a life-changing trek to a homeless camp or a mission trip to a third world country, we promise to never forget. But the definition of true need all too soon fades from our memory when we return to life as usual, relentlessly immersed in a culture of excess. Barraged with advertisement proclaiming need for the latest and greatest, the biggest and best, the nicest and newest of every earthly good. Our eyes are drawn to the magnetic distraction of bright lights and shiny objects paraded before us. We forget the less fortunate while fawning over fame and fortune. With elastic memory, our focus snaps back to what we don't have instead of what we do.

Is it hopeless? Are we destined to succumb to the wooing of the material culture?

Just before His arrest and ultimately, His crucifixion, Jesus prayed for His disciples. "I have given them your word and the world has hated them, for they are not of the world any more than I am of the world. My prayer is not that you take them out of the world but that you protect them from the evil one. They are not of the world, even as I am not of it," John 17:14-16. This portion of Jesus' prayer is often summed up to say, "we must be in the world but not of the world." This phrase can get tossed around like so much other Christian jargon. It's difficult to discern the meaning, the practical application.

Though it may sound appealing, the path to being unaffected by the world's system is not to hermit away from all human contact. Likewise, isolation in a bubble of believers is not the solution. Jesus specifically said He wasn't asking God to remove His disciples from the world. That would directly contradict His command for us to go into the world and preach the gospel, as well as His statement in John 17:18, "As you sent me into the world, I have sent them into the world." He is sending us out to impact the world, but not to be influenced by it.

"Do not conform to the pattern of this world, but be transformed by the renewing of your mind. Then you will be able to test and approve what God's will is—his good, pleasing and perfect will," Romans 12:2.

We are living in a material world, but I do not have to be a material girl. We are capable of existing in the world without embracing the culture. The world won't stop pedaling its wares—that the extravagant is essential, that anything less than lavish is lack. It keeps talking, but we don't have to listen. We are empowered to control the input, to unsubscribe from the world's conversation. Jesus prayed, "Sanctify them by truth; your word is truth," John 17:17. Replace the false with fact. Renewing our minds is a continuous process, much like dying daily. Every day, we must drown out the lies of the world with the truth of God's Word.

Give Generously

My call was transferred to voicemail, so I left the realtor a message. I was smitten with that country home. My husband and I were making an offer—exactly the advertised asking price. I was surprised by the returned response asking for our highest and best offer. We are pretty straightforward people. What you see is what you get. I thought the price had been set; we offered that price. Wasn't the rest formality? Apparently, I did not understand the negotiation game of real estate. A price set high, countered by a low-ball offer, eventually, two parties meet in the middle.

Sometimes we approach God's command to give like a negotiation. We give as little as we think we can get away with, crossing our fingers that He won't come back asking for more. Oh, but God doesn't play games. He wants our firstfruits, not our leftovers. We are expected to bring our highest and best right out of the gate. Let's offer it up the first time. I sure don't want to be the one who hears from God, "Is that all you got?"

We must never forget. All that we are and all that we have is a gift from God and belongs to God. We cannot hold back from Him what is already His. "'Will a mere mortal rob God? Yet you rob me. But you ask, "How are we robbing you?" In tithes and offerings,'" Malachi 3:8.

There's debate among Christians concerning how much we should give. Is 10% necessary, or is it a suggestion? Is it based on gross income or net? Was the command under the law and now we're under grace?

"I do not believe one can settle on how much we ought to give. I am afraid the only safe rule is to give more than we can spare. In other words, if our expenditure on comforts, luxuries, amusements, etc., is up to standard common among those with the same income as our own, we are probably giving away too little. If our charities do not at all pinch or hamper us, I should say they are too small. There ought to be things we should like to do and cannot do because our charities expenditure excludes them." –C.S. Lewis[1]

The moral of the story is this: the debate is futile when we realize we've been wasting our breath asking the wrong question. While trying to narrow down just how much we *have to* give, all along we ought to have been asking how much we *have* to give. Instead of considering how much we must give; let's consider how much we can give. The question is not the minimum we are required to give, but the maximum we are enabled to give.

The line between want and need seems blurred. I cannot define it for you or make a list enumerating the difference. Honestly, want versus need may look different for every one of us. But there is Someone capable of making the line clear and administering individual definitions. I read about a missionary who felt guilty for indulging on chewing gum when he saw other people in need. That may seem too far for us, but if we are honest, most of us have a little wiggle room. If we truly want to know, if we are bold enough to ask, God will reveal what luxuries deemed necessities inhibit our giving.

I giggled like a little girl when we stepped into the ice cream shop for the first time. Gleaming black and white checkered floor tiles met chrome bar stools with red leather seats. Oldies jammin' in the background, I couldn't help but bop along. Behind the counter, a pony-tailed teenager in a candy-cane striped apron greeted us with a cheer. I stepped up to the chrome-trimmed counter. "Two scoops of salted caramel for me, please." The young lady seemed proud of her creation as she thrust my cone forward. "That'll be $6." There in her outstretched hand was a sugar cone topped with two golf ball sized scoops of ice cream.

"Give, and it will be given to you. A good measure, pressed down, shaken together and running over, will be poured into your lap. For with the measure you use, it will be measured to you," Luke 6:38.

In this verse, Jesus urges us not to be stingy. After all, the size of the scoop you use to dish it out, will also be the scoop used to serve you. So let's throw out the teaspoon and dig in deep with a snow shovel! Don't give little. Give Big!

You may be following what I am saying about giving generously, but all the same, you cannot help feeling your contribution is pretty small. Take heart! We find in Matthew

10:42, "And if anyone gives even a cup of cold water to one of these little ones who is my disciple, truly I tell you, that person will certainly not lose their reward." You see, it's not the size of the gift that matters. A generous gift for one may not look the same for another. In Acts 11:29, the church was commended for giving, not each one the same amount, but "as each one was able."

"Jesus sat down opposite the place where the offerings were put and watched the crowd putting their money into the temple treasury. Many rich people threw in large amounts. But a poor widow came and put in two very small copper coins, worth only a few cents. Calling his disciples to him, Jesus said, 'Truly I tell you, this poor widow has put more into the treasury than all the others. They all gave out of their wealth; but she, out of her poverty, put in everything—all she had to live on,'" Mark 12:41-44.

The story of the widow's mite reaffirms. We may not think we have much to offer, but God looks at the size of our hearts, not the size of our gifts. Jesus was not impressed by the one who gave the largest sum, but the one who made the largest sacrifice. Let's follow the widow's example. Be generous. Put. It. All. In.

Give Good

I know we've heard one man's trash is another man's treasure, but giving trash and expecting it to be treasured is not blessing. Despite the popular adage, it is not the thought that counts; how we give and what we give matters.

In the final book of the Old Testament, the word of the Lord came to Israel through the prophet, Malachi. In chapter one, verse six the people were called out for their lack of honor and respect. "Sacrifices were inferior. Tithes were neglected." "Their offering of diseased and blemished animals, which they would not have dared to offer to their

119

governor, was in reality an insult to God."[2] –Halley's Bible Handbook

"'But you ask, "How have we shown contempt for your name?" By offering defiled food on my altar,'" Malachi 1:6b-7a.

"Defiled food?" Cringe. That sounds like cleaning out the cupboard during a food drive and giving away all the expired food along with that random can of lima beans accidentally grabbed while mindlessly reaching for corn in the grocery aisle.

God was straight forward with the Israelites about the consequences of subpar offerings. He said in Malachi 2:2b, "I will curse your blessing." God is not honored when we try to pass off our scraps as sacrifice or call our trash a tithe. He makes it clear. That is not participating in the Blessing Cycle; the blessing is cursed.

"Which of you, if your son asks for bread, will give him a stone? Or if he asks for a fish, will give him a snake? If you, then, though you are evil, know how to give good gifts to your children, how much more will your Father in heaven give good gifts to those who ask him! So in everything, do to others what you would have them do to you, for this sums up the Law and the Prophets," Matthew 7:9-12.

When I heard "do unto others," in elementary school, it meant don't call names and don't cut in line. In context, Jesus is telling us—our Father God gives us good gifts, and we like getting good gifts. So, we should give good because God gives good.

Whether it is a gift giving occasion, passing on hand-me-downs, or donating to charity, there are three ways to be sure to give good:

Consider. Remember. Inquire.

Consider: I savored the last sip of hazelnut coffee, holding up a finger for Sandy to hold that thought as I stepped into her garage to pitch my cup. I took in a deep breath, and it came out in a huff. In plain sight, on the very top of the trash-filled can was a shiny red box, cellophane still intact. It was the gift I had given Sandy's three-year-old son for his birthday only two weeks earlier. If you know me at all, it would be no surprise, I was tempted to reach into the trash and rescue the unappreciated gift. Instead, I tossed my cup on top and marched back to the porch. I didn't utter a peep about what I saw, but my saltiness was likely apparent. In my state of offense, I silently vowed to never again buy that ungrateful Sandy or her brat children another gift. Ever.

I held a grudge for a couple of years. In fact, I originally wrote this story in *To Don't,* illustrating not expecting gratitude. But as I started digging into how we ought to give, I realized, the issue of the discarded present wasn't the receiver, it was the gift and even more so, the giver.

We had gathered in the same garage among red balloons and silver streamers a couple of Saturdays before. Sandy clapped her hands as her little boy tore open the brightly colored wrapping paper. "Say cheese!" The snap and flash were Sandy's next cue. "Jordan, what do you say to Cassia?" They cheered in unison, "Thank you!" So how did my unopened gift end up headed for the landfill? As I think back, the gift was, in fact, appreciated; it simply wasn't appropriate. You see, I had not considered whether 1,000 of the world's tiniest stickers would be a blessing to a mother with two rambunctious toddlers. I didn't even buy the gift because I thought Jordan would like it. I snatched the box of stickers off the clearance rack while rushing through the grocery store on my way to the party. Bargain shopping is my jam. It is totally acceptable to get a good deal on a good gift. But that's not what I did. I thoughtlessly dropped a few bucks on something to fill a gift obligation. Giving good gifts means considering what the other person would like to receive, not only what I want to give.

Asa often asked if we could volunteer at the thrift shop ministry. Never lacking donations, the greatest need was sorting through mounds of boxes and garbage bags. Much of what we sorted ended up in the trash. Headless Barbie dolls, teddy bears with missing eyes, broken crayons and random puzzle pieces. Who thinks giving a soiled, stretched out, holey T-shirt is blessing? The ministry was burdened, not blessed by those donations.

Before tossing something into the give-away bin, we need to consider whether an item is worth donating. Would it be an insult if given to me? Would I give it to a family member? Instead of giving trash for someone else to throw away, we can cut out the middle-man and dispose of it ourselves.

Remember: What little girl doesn't squeal at her first ever birthday party invitation? The instant I opened the envelope, I knew the gift I would give. From the moment my eyes had met her painted-on blue eyes in the toy aisle at Kmart, I had been dreaming of one particular Strawberry Shortcake doll. The circular opening in the clear plastic front of her box invited me to take in the sweet strawberry scent of her silky red hair. Every shooting star, wishbone, and blown out candle from that time on was spent wishing I would get that doll or one of her fruit pastry friends for the next special occasion. The purchase was a sacrifice for my mom, but she let me choose a thoughtful, generous gift, to teach me thoughtful, generous giving. I wiggled in my chair, wide-eyed, grinning like a Cheshire cat as the birthday girl opened my gift. I just knew she would love it as much as I would have.

That afternoon, as girls ran from room to room giggling, I beamed to see the birthday girl holding my perfect gift in her hand. She caught a glimpse of my smile and smirked, "This doll is stupid!" Then, she gave the toy a toss. I caught a whiff of Strawberry Shortcake's sweet berry scent as she flew past me, her body going one way and her pink pleated hat the other. When the doll hit the floor, so did my heart.

I'm not telling you this because you have been cordially invited to join my pity party. I had forgotten the story all together until one Sunday morning nearly a decade and a half later. My sister-in-law, Holly and I lingered in the church lobby waiting for the rest of our family to arrive. Because people change considerably, I was surprised to recognize the birthday girl I hadn't seen since kindergarten. Remembering the party incident, I told Holly the Strawberry Shortcake story and quickly forgot it again.

Early in April, my family gathered at my parent's house to over-indulge on the best lasagna ever. As I shoveled in one last bite, my brother handed me a package. As my finger slid through the scotch tape, releasing the comic strip paper from the back of the box, my heart melted and began to drip down my cheek. My eyes once again met the painted-on blue eyes of that sweet-smelling Strawberry Shortcake doll.

At the age of 20, I was no longer pining away for a 1980's cartoon character. Oh, but that gift was a treasure. Holly remembered my story and gave me more than a doll. It was the gift of a beautiful new memory. As I recount the story to put it to paper now, my melting heart threatens to spill out onto my cheek once again.

Inquire: In the midst of cleaning out my closets, I learned most other people have an overflowing supply of their own. If her daughter's closet is already packed with clothes that never get worn, more clothes might be unwanted. If it looks like the library exploded in their toy room, more books may not be a blessing. A heaping bag of hand-me-downs can weigh down hearts as well as arms. Finding new homes for someone else's discards is a burden, not a blessing. This inconvenience is avoidable by asking, "Would you like to look through the clothes my child has outgrown?" Inquiring before giving affords the recipient the freedom to decline or choose just the few items they could actually use.

We may need help knowing how to give a good gift, but inquiring can be tricky. This is a good place to remember: ADOPT. ADAPT. ADLIB. It's important to know our audience so as not to offend. Some may consider it tacky to ask a straight-up question like "What do you want for your birthday?" Others posed with the same question may hand you a list. Especially when asking adults, the question is often shot down, "Oh, you don't need to get me anything." Here are a few ways to inquire to ensure we give good:

- Ask indirectly during casual conversation. "I love Italian food; Macaroni Grill is our absolute favorite. What's your top restaurant pick?"
- Ask someone else. A spouse, child, parent, or friend may have a good idea of what someone wants or needs.
- Ask for a list. After Thanksgiving dinner, my cousins and I would gather around the JC Penney catalog to make our wish lists. Grandma made sure at least a few of those items would be under the tree on Christmas Eve. We can also ask in a roundabout way. "What's on your Christmas list this year?"
- Let them pick. A gift card may seem impersonal, but letting the receiver choose ensures the gift will be good. Treating someone to a shopping trip is a double-dipper. It gives a personally chosen gift and creates the opportunity to make a memory.

Give at Home

When I pay the bill for the stranger behind me in the drive-thru, that's blessing. When I pay for my son's meal, that's lunch. How do we bless our families through giving? Of course, we give gifts on birthdays and holidays, but meeting our families' material needs can feel like part of our job description.

It's worth repeating—the heart of blessing is having a heart to bless. We can approach day-to-day things like grocery shopping motivated to fill the cart and pantry, or we can be intentional to choose items our people will enjoy. Honestly, I've done it both ways. When I choose one of my husband's favorites, something we haven't had in a while, I may enjoy it more than he does because my heart was set to bless him.

I pick up a little gift here or there—a new shirt, a surprise toy. But giving is not always about spending money. My 6'5" hunk of a man requires a lot of fuel. Add a teenage nearly-man, and I am hard-pressed to keep enough food in the house. For me, giving is often handing over half of my meal when they've scarfed theirs down and ask, "Is there more?" My husband always gets the best steak, the biggest slice of pie, and if there's only one piece of cherry cheesecake left, it's his. Asa gets to lick cake batter from beaters, finish off the cool whip, and he usually gets the second biggest everything. Giving at home sometimes means sacrificing our own material desires and even needs for those of our family.

Good Stewards

A wealthy man was scheduled to fly out of the country on an extended business trip. Before leaving, he assembled his top three employees, asking them to manage his affairs while he was gone. To the first, he entrusted 2.5 million dollars; to the second, 1 million dollars; to the third, half a million dollars. When the businessman returned from his trip, he again gathered his top three employees to evaluate the management of his funds. The first employee reported, "Sir, you entrusted me with 2.5 million dollars. I invested your money and added 2.5 million more." "Well done," replied the employer. "Your hard work has earned you a promotion and a hefty bonus." The second employee chimed in, "You gave me 1 million dollars, and I doubled it." "Well done. You, too, will be promoted, and there's a bonus check with your name on it." The businessman looked to the third employee, "Well?" "Sir, I didn't want to lose your money, so I stuffed it under my mattress. You still have the entire half million." The employers' jaw clenched, as he spit out, "You're fired!"

The story above uses current day terms to relate "The Parable of the Talents" told by Jesus in Matthew 25. Everything belongs to God, so we're not really owners of our money and material possessions. We're more like managers or administrators of God's resources. He has entrusted us to act on His behalf, to properly manage His possessions according to His will. Handling God's things responsibly is being a good steward. Just like the employees in the parable, we will be held accountable for how we manage what God has given us. This important principle is not exclusive to how we spend and save our money, but also how we give it.

We must give generously, but we cannot give flippantly. All charities are not created equal. Many organizations, some of what we think of as household names in do-gooding, even those claiming to be Christian, mishandle donations. Funds may be wasted, pocketed, or used to fund activities that are not honoring to God. Worse yet, some "charities" are outright scams; none of the money collected goes to bless anyone. A good steward is an educated giver; we must do our homework to ensure we support legitimate causes that do not support activities in opposition to Scripture. We need to know where our money goes, but there is an important balance between caution and cynicism. Let's not become stingy while guarding against being swindled. If we do our best to research reputable organizations, we ultimately need to trust God with the outcome.

As a young adult, being equally swept up by emotional manipulation and the distortion of God's Word, I was an avid consumer of false-teaching disguised as gospel. Coerced by high-pressure sales pitches, I pledged monthly donations to a number of so-called ministries. Eventually, my monthly commitment totaled more than my pay before any bills were paid. I sent check after check with pledge cards, believing God would send a windfall to cover the rest. When I got dangerously behind financially, I realized, something had to give. God did not bail me out of my fiscal crisis, because He had not asked me to give beyond my means. We must guard against giving emotionally. "Each of you should give what you have decided in your heart to give, not reluctantly or under compulsion," 2 Corinthians 9:7a. Being pushed into giving is not good stewardship. Generous giving must be the result of Spirit motivation, not manipulation. God will often stir in our hearts to give generously, sacrificially, sometimes astonishingly so. If we are led by the Spirit to give, we cannot out-give God. There is a distinct difference between conviction and compulsion. If we are led by emotion, God is under no obligation to repay our foolishness.

Always be prepared

"We would like you to travel to Greenville next week." Rarely had anyone with my job description been sent on a business trip; it had never happened to me before. Knowing there were more qualified people who should go, I reasoned God must have a purpose in the invitation. "Make me a blessing, Lord. Reveal the reason I am being sent."

I enjoyed the two-and-a-half-hour drive to my appointment. Most of the time I spent talking to God, making a joyful noise along to worship music. It was like getting paid for a date with Jesus. Arriving at the facility, I eagerly looked for God's purpose. My knowledge was barely a contribution to the scheduled meeting. I figured that must not have been my mission. A former boss shared some career advice, which happened to be in direct opposition to how I felt God was leading me. "Was I wrong, Lord? Did you bring me here to change my direction?" That didn't seem to be the reason either. I left the plant bewildered.

After just half an hour on the road headed home, I had to make an urgent stop. Crossing one's legs is a difficult maneuver when driving. While I was in the restroom, I heard the in-unison crying of a woman and a toddler. I prayed right where I was. "Dear Lord, please minister in this situation." I hurried out and caught the young mother in the hallway. "How can I help you?" The toddler quieted as the tear-stained twenty-something girl explained. On the way across state to visit her failing grandmother in the hospital, she was nearly out of gas and totally out of money. After offering to fill her tank, I followed the grey minivan two miles to the closest gas station. I swiped my card, smiled, and turned to leave when the young mom shouted. "Wait! Just before you approached me, I was on the phone asking my dad what to do. He told me to pray, and I said, 'What's God going to do?' But I decided to try. I prayed thinking it wouldn't do any good, then there you were."

BAM! God's perfect placement and sublime scheduling were made evident in that Blessing Appointed Moment. The purpose of my business trip was not business at all. He arranged in advance to send me 137 miles from my home, to be at the exact place at the precise time, to answer a prayer the very moment it was prayed.

God has a purpose for where He has placed you today. Don't be afraid to reach out. You never know when you have been set up to be a blessing in answer to someone else's prayer.

I didn't know my way around the big city. Thank God for GPS. "In 1000 feet, turn right." Growing up in farm country, I had rarely seen a homeless person. And as I told you before, when I did, I usually kept scrolling. But at that moment when I noticed the woman on the curb with a sign in her hand, tires squealed as I slammed the car to an abrupt halt mid-street. I left the driver side door hanging wide open and scurried to the back hatch of my SUV. Snatching up our bag of snacks, I rushed across two lanes of traffic to hand over all the food we had brought on our road trip. Returning to the car, I snapped my seatbelt as the door slammed shut. "Mom! What were you thinking?" Yes, my son was right. In my zeal to be a blessing, my rash actions were unwise and unsafe.

In recent years, our travels have brought us more frequent encounters with homeless people. Though not as bad as parking mid-street and dodging traffic, more than once, horns honked as I held up traffic while scrambling for an emergency protein bar to toss out the window. After a few near-misses, I realized I should plan ahead. My son and I decided to assemble "Blessing Bags." I picked up a few drawstring backpacks, and we filled them with things like hand warmers, trail mix, beef jerky. Asa was excited to find pocket-sized Bibles to add. The bags hang nicely on the headrest in the car, so now, rather than scrambling and holding up traffic, we are prepared to bless.

On my way into the grocery store, I frowned at the woman ringing the bell. "Sorry, I don't carry cash." It wasn't an excuse; it was the honest truth. I genuinely felt bad saying "No." After scanning the last item on the belt, the cashier asked, "Would you like cash back?" Before I could say "No," like I usually did, the Holy Spirit butted right into our conversation. Saying "Yes" eliminated my reason for not giving. Since then, I try to keep a little cash on hand so I am prepared to give.

With blessing bags hanging from the seat and a little stash of cash, you'd think I would be completely prepared to give. But perhaps what needs to be prepared most is not the gift to be given, but the heart of the giver.

Give Joyfully

"For God loves a cheerful giver," 2 Corinthians 9:7b.

From a little white church on a quiet country hillside, lively praise echoes for miles. The pastor reminds: "Give Generously. Give Joyfully." Shouts of joy, "WooHoo!" and "Amen!" resound as bills, coins, checks, and envelopes drop into the passing plates.

There is not a magic formula, no tip or trick to giving joyfully. It all comes down to this simple fact: we get to choose our attitude. We can choose to have a poverty mindset—a constant fear of lack that makes giving painful. We can choose to settle on a greed mentality—believing we have worked hard for everything we have and don't owe anyone else a thing. Or we can choose an attitude of gratitude—counting our blessings and remembering what a privilege it is to participate in the Blessing Cycle. If we aren't feeling like "it is more blessed to give than to receive,"[3] we already have a few weapons in our arsenal to help us get there.

Be persistent in prayer. James 4:2b says, "You do not have because you do not ask God." If we are not experiencing joy in giving, let's ask God to give it to us. We know He answers prayers according to His will, and no doubt, He wants us to give joyfully.

Be immersed in God's Word. Let's remind ourselves what God's Word says about giving. Memorize it. Repeat it. Post it. I taped some verses right at the point of use—inside my wallet and on my checkbook—so I can see them when I spend and give

Put. It. On. The principle we learned in *Encourage* applies to *Give* as well. Put on a smile. Behave joyfully as we give. Be intentional until it becomes instinctual.

When we truly have a heart to bless; when we see our offerings blessing others; when we remember even though He does not need us, our Father is allowing us to participate in His Blessing Cycle; joy will surely follow.

Lord, thank You for the opportunity to participate in Your Blessing Cycle through giving. Please show me my own unique "such as I have"—what You have given me in extra supply so that I may bless others. Lead me in generous giving, and allow me to be a good steward of all You have given me. Help me to give good gifts as You have so abundantly blessed me with good gifts. Birth within my spirit an unspeakable joy as I give according to Your will. In Jesus name, amen.

CHAPTER 6

Serve

Meet Physical Needs

♪Be to the helpless a helper indeed,

Unto the mission be true. ♪

"Everybody can be great, because anybody can serve. You don't have to have a college degree to serve. You don't have to make your subject and verb agree to serve. You only need a heart full of grace. A soul regenerated by love."
–Dr. Martin Luther King Jr.[1]

Don't Put Serve in a Box

Serve is the one blessing package where I am most tempted to label myself and limit God. Service shrinks down to fit neatly in my imaginary box. I narrow what counts as serving and determine anything outside my definition doesn't qualify. I over-think it, over-complicate it. In *Pray,* we talked about being eager to *do* something to be a blessing because we are people of action. I arrived here at *Serve*, the action-y-est part of being made a blessing, and before I even got started, I was overwhelmed to the point of inaction. Paralyzed by the question, "What does service really look like?"

The book of James paints a picture of a double-minded person. They are "like a wave of the sea, blown and tossed by the wind," and "unstable in all they do."[2] That right there, friends, is the CliffsNotes version of my life. Just when I've made up my mind, I'm sloshed violently to the other side. My scattered thoughts go something like this:

I'm only doing what's important; dream big dreams for God.

The small things right in front of me should be my sole focus.

Service means only activities that support my calling.

If I don't sign up for everything, I'll miss my opportunity.

The mundane tasks at home are a distraction from real service.

Home is my exclusive role; I have no time to serve elsewhere.

Service only counts if it is connected to the church.

My church has no place for me to serve.

I want to do everything.

I only want to do specific things.

I don't want to do anything.

The back and forth leaves me seasick. One problem with a narrow definition is we get stuck with an either/or scenario.

I'm *either* supposed to serve in big ways *or* in small ways. *Either* I have a calling, *or* I serve wherever needed. *Either* in my home *or* outside. *Either* church *or* other places.

My friend needed a break. "What if there's a season when I don't serve?" The answer is: there will be seasons when our service looks different. At certain times we might not be on anyone's roster as a dedicated volunteer, but that doesn't mean we're not serving. *Serve* is blessing others by meeting physical needs. When we accept this broader definition of service, we understand that we inherently serve others in many ways, whether we're officially signed up for it or not.

Often, we are called to serve inside the confines of our preconceived ideas. But other times the opportunity to serve is unexpected—outside the box. The truth is, we can't put serve in an either/or box because it is both/and. We are called to do *both* big things *and* small things. *Both* in our calling *and* where needed. *Both* at home *and* at church *and* everywhere else God directs. Both/and does not mean trying to do it all. It means service is not defined by one or the other, and it may look different from season to season.

"We can't help everyone, but everyone can help someone." –Ronald Reagan[3]

Here's some of the best advice I ever received: "Under commit and over deliver." I've had a tendency to do the opposite, to take on so much I could rarely manage to fit it all in. There are countless opportunities for good works that contribute to the kingdom, but not every good work is my work. God already has a plan. We are equipped to do the specific activities He prepared in advance.

Practically speaking, how do we choose our own assignments? Some of us follow our hearts. But the truth is, our emotions lie. "The heart is deceitful above all things and beyond cure. Who can understand it?" Jeremiah 17:9. Since we cannot trust our hearts, many of us use our heads. We rely on logic to figure out what makes sense, what fits in our schedules, what best suits us, what ultimately serves us. Our hearts lead us with emotion, but our heads drive us to ambition. Frankly, we cannot count on our hearts or our heads to point us in the right direction. Choosing our own assignments only happens when we are led, not by emotion or ambition, but solely by the Spirit. This means continually returning to the foundations of being persistent in prayer and immersed in God's Word.

The Best Example

When I am tossed about, the only way to regain center is to fix my eyes squarely on Jesus. One of the most poignant examples of how to serve, truly how to live, is in chapter 13 of the Gospel of John. Maybe you're familiar with the time at the Last Supper when Jesus washed the disciples' feet. Hold on right there for a moment. Feet are gross. Even today—with high-tech, breathable shoes and foot powder and lotion and toenail clippers and mani-pedis—feet are disgusting. But back in Jesus' day, feet were a whole 'nother level of nasty. On foot was the main mode of transportation. Despite what we may have seen in an Easter play, Peter, James, and John did not wear Birkenstock's. With rudimentary sandals at best, these pedestrians walked the same dusty roads traveled by horses and donkeys—animals indiscriminate about where they relieve themselves. The dehumanizing task of foot washing was reserved for the lowliest of servants.

Jesus was *big time*. He spoke to multitudes; basically, He packed out stadiums. But Jesus wasn't just a paparazzi magnet; He is, in fact, God incarnate. If anyone ever had the right to be self-important, to think any menial task was beneath Him, it would have been Jesus. But, the King of Kings got up in the middle of dinner, tied a towel around His waist, and without even cringing, cupped in His hand a filthy, calloused, jagged-toe-nailed foot. This selfless act of service was so audacious that Peter protested. How could he possibly allow Jesus to abase Himself in such a way?

Jesus was redefining leadership. He explained the world's system says greatness is power and position and making a name for yourself. But God's way says, "Whoever wants to become great among you must be your servant," Matthew 20:26b. Jesus Himself "did not come to be served, but to serve, and to give His life as a ransom for many," Matthew 20:28b.

Jesus isn't a supervisor; He is a leader. He isn't an instructor; He's a teacher. Jesus didn't just tell the disciples what to do; He showed them. And then sometimes He followed up the demonstration with an explanation because, just like me, the disciples were often slow to get the point. They needed to have it all spelled out for them. In John 13 verses 12 and 15, Jesus said, "Do you understand what I have done for you? I have set you an example that you should do as I have done for you."

When we ask for the assignments we prefer, none of us is begging to do the disgusting and difficult and dehumanizing. No, we want to do what is fun and easy, and honestly, what might get some recognition. Sickness of self still lingers. We want to be elevated, not humbled. We want an important position, not one of servitude. We make service all about us. But true service is a sacrifice of our time, energy, abilities, and most of all our pride. A servant's heart requires humility. Jesus did the big and the small, the important and the mundane, what got attention and what went unnoticed. His example of serving well forces me to examine my heart and process the areas where I need to be more like Him and less like me.

Lord, thank you for Jesus' selfless example of blessing others through service. Teach me to live like Him. As I navigate choosing my own assignments, may I be led, not by emotion or ambition, but solely by Your Spirit.

Before we move on, there's one little nugget of truth at the end of this passage I don't want us to miss. After washing the disciple's feet and encouraging us all to follow His example, Jesus said, "Now that you know these things, you will be blessed if you do them," John 13:17. This is the Blessing Cycle! He essentially expressed: be a blessing; be blessed.

Bailiwick

In the hallway just outside of the staff meeting, I bumped into my boss. Literally. I never watch where I'm going. I thanked him for the recent assignment I had been given. "No problem," he replied. "I thought it was right up your bailiwick." He walked ahead into the meeting, and I muttered under my breath, "Up your bailiwick!" Honestly, I hadn't heard that term before, so as soon as the meeting was over, I snatched the dictionary from my desk drawer to look it up. Apparently, it was a compliment. He meant this new project was right in line with my particular area of interest and expertise. In my element, my wheelhouse. It was my jam. Now that makes more sense.

You are gifted. I wonder if this is the first time you have been told that truth. Or maybe you have heard it enough times that the words have lost their meaning. My Grandma Phyllis spoke those words over me more times than she said my name, but I figured it was her love-colored glasses talking. Every grandparent thinks their grandkid is next in line to win the Nobel Prize. Maybe you struggle to recognize your giftedness too. We each have our own unique bailiwick of blessing comprised of three parts: Spiritual Gifts, talents, and skills. When we are in Christ, the Holy Spirit of God takes up residence inside of us and empowers each one with different Spiritual Gifts. Talents are natural abilities, something you just seem to have a knack for. Skills are learned abilities, a craft we have been taught or an acquired aptitude.

As we are sorting out living with humility and being others-focused, acknowledging our gifts may seem counter to the mission. Talking about how much we have to offer does sound a little self-centered. After all, we don't want to be the Grand Marshall of our own parade. John 3:27 helps us keep this in perspective. "A person can receive only what is given them from heaven." Whether Spiritual Gifts, talents, or skills, all of our contributions ultimately spring from the same Source. They are unmerited blessings endowed on us by God. A kind of "such as I have."

What is your bailiwick of blessing? Take an inventory. Discover your Spiritual Gifts. Document your talents and skills. This exercise is not taking stock of what we think is great about ourselves. It is enumerating the many abilities God has blessed us with for use in His service. These gifts are a continuation of our Count Your Blessings List. So don't deny it. Don't be afraid to acknowledge how blessed you are. Repeat this truth out loud with me. "I am gifted."

1 Corinthians 12:7 reminds us why these gifts are given. "For the common good." Considering our gifts, talents, and skills can give us direction for work in serving. It's a starting point to begin praying and brainstorming. "How can I use this gift to be a blessing?" We don't have to have it all figured out. God already has that covered. Our role is to recognize our gifts, be watchful for opportunities to use the gifts, and concede to God's plan.

In the New Testament, we find two letters written to Timothy by his mentor Paul. In the first letter, Paul advised, "Do not neglect your gift."[4] He sounds an awful lot like Grandma Phyllis. She often followed up, "You are gifted," by telling me, "You know, God gave you that mind for a reason, so you could use it. He doesn't want you wasting it!"

Your bailiwick of blessing has significant value. These gifts are not our own, and we are called to be good stewards of them. That's not a command to be taken lightly. We have a responsibility to highly regard our gifts and put them to use for the glory of God. In his second letter to Timothy, Paul took it a step further by charging, "fan into flame the gift of God, which is in you."[5] Yes! Keep your gift in play, and don't let it go to waste! But that is not enough. Be all in. Use it to the fullest extent. Ignite that little spark into a passion for blessing. Turn up the heat! Fire it up! Fuel the flame! Set it ablaze!

In a continuation of the same thought, Paul says this in the following verse, "For God gave us a spirit not of fear but of power and love and self-control."[6]

Timothy needed this reminder, and so do we. Fear is a cold wet blanket that smothers the flame and quenches our fire. It tries to hold us back from fully exercising our gifts. It's true, we cannot do it on our own, but we are empowered to go beyond our own strength by the Holy Spirit of the living God.

Lord, thank You for Your many blessings, particularly the gifts, talents, and skills You have given me. Please bring those to my mind as I take an inventory. Help me to not only use my gifts but to fan them into flame as I discover the ways to bring You glory by being made a blessing.

Seek to Serve

"Do small things with great love." –Mother Teresa[7]

My son is the chairman of a one-man door-holding ministry. I typically hold a door open for the person directly behind me in a public venue. But Asa has a mission to conquer every closed door and man his station indefinitely in case there's someone in the zip code who may desire to enter or exit. Common courtesy has become so uncommon in our society, it often catches people off guard.

Yes. This is small. But it is service. There is no quota for what qualifies. Jesus shattered our man-made quotas and qualifications: by using one boy's lunch to feed the 5,000; by acknowledging the widow's mite; by telling us giving a cup of water does not go unnoticed.

Service is not exclusive to our strong suits or scheduled events with a sign-up sheet. There are endless opportunities in our paths every day. Titus 3:14 tells us to devote ourselves to good works. How can we make sure not to miss those opportunities right in front of us? The same concepts we used to Give Good will also help us to Serve Well.

Consider. Remember. Inquire.

Consider: We were wrapping up Bible study when I caught a glimpse of her across the room. The mombie: part mom, part zombie. One is easily recognized by the spit up on her shoulder, messy bun in her hair (but not in a cute way), and the dark circles under her eyes being the only color on her face. We had celebrated her with a baby shower just a few months back, and I could not wait to hear about her couple-week-old boy. "How's the baby?" I cheered. My overexuberance didn't faze her. Remaining expressionless, her head turned toward me in an eerily slow motion. "He screams." I was grateful when the awkward moment was broken by the mother of some college-aged kids who squeezed in between us. She slipped a piece of paper into the new mom's hand. "Call me this week. I'll come hold the baby, and you can take a shower or take a nap or go to the grocery store or rock out to tunes in your car for an hour. Whatever you want. I'll be over."

Think about when you were a new mom, new to the neighborhood, newly divorced? Pull from your own experiences to reach out to people who are currently living where you once were. What blessed you then? Put yourself in the other person's shoes. What do you hope someone would do to help?

Remember: My heart ached to leave our little microfarm. For many years our labor of love was working the land to make our house a home. One of my greatest joys was my thriving raised bed garden. I knew I'd miss the glorious view from our second story bedroom window as the rising sun spilled onto a bounty of vegetables. And I had developed a taste for homegrown produce. But most of all, my garden was the tranquil space where I stuck my hands in the dirt and connected with God.

Planting season would be passed by the time we moved into our new home. Still, I was excited about this little nearly-off-grid log cabin. We met on the front porch with the realtor and our friend Lannie who had built this home years ago. Before the ink was dry on the paper making this home ours, Lannie pointed up the hill. "I planted you a little garden." In freshly tilled earth, rows of tomatoes, cabbage, and peppers peaked above the ground. During one of the many conversations leading up to our home purchase, my left behind garden must have come up. Lannie remembered.

People talk about what's important to them. I am slowly learning to listen more and to talk less, really slowly. When we give someone else air time, we hear what is on their heart. Their wants and needs, their hopes and dreams. We can find out how to be a blessing when we create the space for other people to speak.

Inquire: A devoted wife and busy mom stood tirelessly by the side of her husband's hospital bed as he fought for his life. Responding to an emergency typically means returning to disorder. No one needs the added burden of housework at a time of crisis. God compelled me to go clean their house.

We were in the middle of a drawn-out move, spending half of each week in a different state. I looked around at the chaos in my own home. This place had to be packed and painted and prepped and put on the market. In times not so far past, I would've frantically argued, "What about my own mess?" But

God had been working this *Make Me a Blessing* message in my heart for a while, and I was starting to actually get it. Instead, I whispered, "I know being made a blessing isn't always convenient. Lord, please make a way for me to get everything done."

Every so often God gives us a glimpse of His hand at work in an unmistakable display of the Blessing Cycle. The following day my mom showed up and asked, "How can I help?" She washed my mountain of dishes while I pulled weeds in the landscape. What a sweet reminder of God's perfect plan. A struggling family was blessed; I was blessed in return. My mom was given the opportunity to bless; I am confident the cycle continues so she is blessed as well.

"Let me know if you need anything." Those are words people say when someone is sick or loses a loved one or has any other type of plight. But it doesn't usually mean much; it's small talk. It's like "Bless you" after a sneeze or "How are you today?" We need to be clear that our offer to help is sincere, not just chit-chat. Honestly, sometimes people don't know what we could do to serve them, or they think their need is too much to ask. A good offer of service may include suggesting a specific task. "Does your lawn need mowed? Can I bring you a meal? Do you need a ride?" Inquiring is as tricky in *Serve* as it was in *Give*. We never want to overstep or offend. Knowing our audience can help us ask the right questions.

Serve at Home

I gather a mound of sweaty gym clothes from the bathroom floor (next to, rather than inside, the empty laundry basket). This does not feel like blessing. I scrape last night's crusty green beans from a dinner plate. This does not feel like blessing. I pay bills and plan meals and schedule appointments

143

and do a million other mundane activities every single day. None of this feels like blessing. Especially when all the tedious chores seem to go unnoticed and unappreciated. Plus, this housekeeping stuff is keeping me from doing important things for God.

"Lord, nobody even sees everything I do around here. Is a little appreciation too much to ask?" Mid pity party is when God reminded me: "Do what's right because it's right to do." I would need more than just my fingers and toes to count the number of times I heard my human father say those same words; the two of them like to team up on me. Dad always added, "And do it right, with the right attitude." This echoes the truth in Colossians 3:22-25 (MSG): "Servants, do what you're told by your earthly masters. And don't just do the minimum that will get you by. Do your best. Work from the heart for your real Master, for God, confident that you'll get paid in full when you come into your inheritance. Keep in mind always that the ultimate Master you're serving is Christ. The sullen servant who does shoddy work will be held responsible. Being Christian doesn't cover up bad work."

I want to serve my family well, with excellence, with the right attitude. When I go through the motions of meeting my loved ones' needs without setting my heart on blessing them, I fall short. I want to be intentional about blessing my family, and I also want to serve them with joy. It's easy for me to talk: "Like every other blessing package, *Serve* begins in our homes." But honestly, it is much more difficult for me to walk.

The heart of blessing is having a heart to bless. It's true for serving too. The heart of serving is having a heart to serve. Those words sound right as I type them. However, in the messiness of real life, these sentiments seem to echo back empty. If I am to be effective in serving, I need a servant's heart. But how do I go about getting it? Is a servant's heart simply a matter of choice? Are there action steps I take to develop it? I am desperate for practical application. Where is the bridge I cross to take my heart from underwhelmed to overjoyed as I serve in my home?

My go-to is to place blame. I slipped in a remark here and there to remind my family of all I do for them. I asked God to help them notice my contribution, to make them more grateful, then I could be content in serving my people. And suddenly I realized the root of my struggle was self-focus. It's easier to help strangers and even give them a pass on acknowledging my efforts. But I was still holding my family to expectations of gratitude and reciprocation. Since I didn't quite feel like they were doing either, I resorted to complaining. The command to serve is not predicated on anyone else's response. Frankly, I knew I was the one in need of a heart change.

Gratitude is the catalyst to being made a blessing. These words preach well, but do they practically apply when I'm elbow-deep in dishwater? I test drove a theory as I folded laundry.

I pulled out a pair of jeans.
Lord, I am grateful for my husband who works hard to provide for our family.

I grabbed a sock and dug around for its mate.
God, thank you that we are blessed financially by Chris's good job.

I slipped a hanger through the neck of a polo shirt.
Thank you, Father, that I can serve my husband by keeping his clothes clean.

It is not magic. But a critical shift in my attitude began. As I continued to intentionally express my own gratitude, I recognized that I wasn't as overlooked as I led myself to believe. My husband swiped his fork across the plate and took one last bite. "Good meal, babe." I dismissed it before because those weren't the exact words I expected in utterance of gratitude. "Those are the best carrots I've ever had! Are there more, Mom?" This is appreciation, and I am convicted because I hadn't noticed it before.

Lord, thank you for supplying us with good food to eat. I am grateful for the opportunity to create meals that provide for the nutritional needs of my family.

We serve God by serving others. When I view every act of caring for my family's physical needs as an act of service to them, and therefore service to God, everything changes. Here comes the Proverbs 31 woman again, always setting the example. Verse 12 says, "Her husband lacks nothing. She will do him good and not evil all the days of her life." Later, verse 15 tells us, "She provides food for her family. Her family is clothed in fine clothes." God made a point to put these acts of service in His Word in the chapter defining a virtuous woman. Caring for the basic, physical needs of our own families is not menial in the eyes of our Father; it is a virtue.

Your family dynamic may not look like mine which means your service may not look like mine. Actually, my family dynamic looked completely different six years ago when I was working outside of my home for 60+ hours a week. I wish I would have known then that I was still blessing and serving my family by meeting their physical needs. I guess I thought because I was less hands-on at home it somehow didn't qualify. My good job allowed me to pay someone else to do the laundry. I was able to nourish my family with food another person cooked. That is no less a blessing. I mean, the Bible says our friend from Proverbs "provides her family with food." It doesn't say she never ordered takeout.

I hope whatever your life looks like, that you can personalize this truth as well. I encourage you to Adopt. Adapt. Adlib. Specific tasks or how they are accomplished are not what matter. When you contribute to the physical needs of those around you, you are blessing. Even when you are fulfilling what seems like an obligation or performing your occupation. You are not unnoticed. You are not unappreciated. God sees; He knows. He gave you your own mission because He values your work. It is important. You make a difference. You are being made a blessing.

I have admitted, I have desperate need for balance. God wants us to stand still, right smack dab in the middle of the teeter-totter. After I fully convinced myself that the tasks I do in my home, to care for my people, somehow qualify as service, I stepped my foot off center and tipped over to the other side. In short order, I was content, deciding my in-home service filled my quota. My busy life as a wife and mom has me constantly teetering back and forth. One day I find it difficult to have a servant's heart in my home and the next I hide behind my family, using them as an excuse to not serve elsewhere.

I took that crumpled "Just a mom" nametag out of the trash, pieced it back together, and slapped it over my heart like I was pledging allegiance to it. I labeled myself a uni-tasker and limited God from using me in any other capacity. In accepting homemaking as my whole-life purpose, I failed to look for my Right Now Purpose.

I saw a quote as I scrolled through social media. Something like, "Your most important contribution to the world may be the person you raise." Powerful words. It was true for Jesus' mother Mary. It was true for John the Baptist's mother Elizabeth. It could quite possibly be true for you and me. Absolutely, the prayer of my heart is that God would use my son to have an impact in the lives of others. Caring for our families is our central role, perhaps even our most important role in the service of our Father. But let's not mistake our *number one* assignment to serve for our *one and only* assignment to serve.

Our steps are ordered by the Lord.[8] Every place we go and every person we encounter sets us up for an opportunity to bless. If I've checked the box of service because I swept the floor and took out the trash today, I may miss the opportunity.

We know seasons will shift the amount of time God uses us to serve in different capacities. But, haven't we teetered on the totter of either/or long enough? Serve is both/and. I can serve effectively in my home and wherever else in my circle of influence that God gives me opportunity.

Serve in Our Church

Besides my own back porch and Marblehead lighthouse, my church is my happy place. Each week I'm directed to the closest parking space by gentlemen in safety-yellow vests who bring umbrellas car-side when it's raining. The doors are swung open by two delightful women; one of them hands me a bulletin. I grab a piping hot cup of freshly brewed coffee before heading into the sanctuary. Worship is led by gifted vocalists and talented musicians before a spot-on message is preached straight from the Word of God. I don't really know how many volunteers it takes to pull off a Sunday service. I guess I don't actually think about it very often. It's easy to get into the groove of being fed and being served. Sometimes we need to be reminded: Ask not what your church can do for you, but what you can do for your church.

I lead a small group at my church. It really doesn't feel like service. I get far more out of it than I put into it. I didn't ask to lead. I showed up at the volunteer table one Sunday after church and introduced myself. I was new to the area and to the church. I rambled on talking about my former home church and the Bible study I used to lead. Maybe I was trying to convince them I was a Christian, or maybe it was the only adult conversation I'd had in the past month. I said, "I'm here on Tuesday night. Is there anything I can do to serve then?" I thought maybe they would let me make coffee or wipe off tables or stack chairs. "We need group leaders." I know I'm called to serve women, so I was good with it.

You know what I'm not good with? Children. It's not that I don't like kids. I'm madly in love with the children in my own family. I just don't like being responsible for the supervision of someone else's children. I'm always afraid I'm going to drop one or lose one or that one of them may spontaneously combust. Children's ministry is not my jam. But every person in my Bible study has agreed to take a turn serving children so everyone gets a chance to attend the group. I'm not a regular, but God gives me opportunities to serve in these one-off situations with kids just often enough to keep me grateful for those He has called to it. My heart for serving women doesn't mean I get a pass on serving all other needs. While Children's Ministry is not my calling, it is occasionally my Right Now Purpose.

"Therefore, as we have the opportunity, let us do good to all people, especially to those who belong to the family of believers," Galatians 6:10.

The verse above is my friend Lannie's favorite one in the whole Bible. It pretty well sums up the way he has lived his life. On Thursday afternoon, he mowed the lawn at the little white church where he had been a member for years. He stopped by the same church late Saturday evening—turning on heat in the winter or air conditioning in the summer—to ensure the sanctuary would be comfortable for the morning service. He never thought his service was a big deal. But it's a big deal to God.

Home is the epicenter of our circle of influence, but our local church is a close second in line. Each church body is different, just like each circle of influence is different, but typically, there is more work than there are workers. I pause from clacking keys, look up at a picture above my desk, and read this quote. "If you want to change the Kingdom, go home and love your church." –Whitney Capps

Interruptions

When I shared the chapter outline for *Make Me a Blessing* with my son, Asa, he said, "I really think you should put *Serve* after *Give* because serving is harder for people." You know, I think he may be right. In our over-scheduled, under-rested lives, we can become stingy with our time. Although the poorest of Americans are wealthier than most of the rest of the world, our culture of incessant busyness has made us one of the poorest peoples when it comes to time equity. All of our modern conveniences have freed up our time and energy so we can fill those moments with even more. We hoard our time, only to fritter it away on activities of no value. Stuff and money are replaceable, but time? The clock is ticking, and time spent can never be retrieved.

There were five items on the agenda that Saturday, with only time for a potty break but not a wardrobe change in between. While wrapping up stop #1, I received the conspicuously vague but loaded text message, "Are you home?" Laura was fishing for a favor. "I'm not home, but my husband may be." Yes, a shameless attempt to pass an inconvenience off on my loved one. (You can hold my "Wife of the Year Award" until the end). Another text came back, this time not so vague. Her son's school project was due in two days; he needed my help.

I realized I had a brief window of free time between activities. To be honest, I didn't want to help, but I knew Laura could see my car in the driveway from her house. She would notice if I was home for very long, so I reluctantly called. "I have an hour until I have to leave for the birthday party if Brian would like to come over to get started on his project." "That's not enough time," she replied. "Really? I'm doing you a **huge** favor squeezing this into my overloaded day, and *you* are refusing because you don't think it's *enough*?" I didn't say those words, but the feeling did underscore my tone when I snipped back, "I understand it's not enough time to complete the entire project, but I could help him get started. And that's all the time I have." Laura's response was the equivalent of "Thanks, but no thanks." Poking one's finger hard on the screen of a smartphone does not bring the satisfaction of the resounding clang created when slamming an old dial-up, ringer phone, but I tried hard to imagine it as I ended the call.

We don't always get mulligans, even when we earnestly pray and sincerely aim to do better the next time, a missed opportunity may never be recovered. But this particular time, God graciously gave me a re-do.

Sunday afternoon I called Laura to offer help if it was still needed. Brian was in the driveway with a notebook in hand before I hung up the phone. His project was to write a paper. Scratched across the top blue line of his first page was the topic: "How to make a difference." Turns out this seemingly ill-timed request was not an interruption at all. It was actually my assignment. Right up my bailiwick. God planned in advance for me to use my gifts of teaching and writing, not just to help complete a school project, but to share the principles of being made a blessing.

If we are serious when asking God to make us a blessing, we have to be willing to sacrifice. Embrace inconveniences. Make room for the unexpected. This *Make Me a Blessing* journey is all about being others-focused. And God is changing our hearts at the same time, making us more like Jesus. God is not surprised by anything that happens during the course of our day. He's sovereign. What we see as an interruption may actually be an intervention to get our plans in alignment with His. "Many plans are in a person's heart, but it is the LORD's purpose that prevails," Proverbs 19:21.

Big Dreams and Small Things

I had a dream. A big dream. My big dream was to write a book; this book, in fact. Functionally, a book is not one big thing. A book is 60,000 small things—words. Words used to express ideas are crafted into sentences, arranged in paragraphs, ordered by chapters, and nestled inside a cover.

Writing this book was itself, only a small part of something bigger, a calling. To use my gifts—to write, speak, and lead—to encourage and inspire women. I don't know how it will all play out. But it started by being obedient in the small. My first assignment using my bailiwick to bless was to publish a monthly newsletter for our homeschool group. This gave families in our community an outlet for communication, and I gained practice, growing in my craft. I was blessed and made a blessing in the same act of service.

My first opportunity to publicly speak God's Word was giving the devotion at a meeting when I was a consultant for Thirty-One Gifts. The message I shared was from Genesis 12:2. "We are blessed to be a blessing." My gifts were not reserved for the Future Promise of my big dream and calling, they had a Right Now Purpose. As I have continued to be faithful in the smaller assignments, fulfilling my Right Now Purpose, I am gradually seeing opportunities getting bigger.

"Whoever can be trusted with very little can also be trusted with much," Luke 16:10a.

God wants us to dream big dreams and undertake great endeavors to further His kingdom. Don't think for a minute doing the small minimizes that. You see, big things are actually made up of many small things.

My blank calendar left an entire afternoon open, dedicated to my big dream. I went back and forth between spending it at my favorite sandwich shop and my favorite coffee shop. A hankering for iced chai won out. I lugged in my big bag of writing implements and settled at a high-top table. First, I would finish an article submission for a Christian magazine, then dive in to the next chapter of *Make Me a Blessing*. I'm a people watcher, and as my husband puts it, I cannot restrain myself from striking up conversation with random people for no apparent reason. I determined to keep my head down and get busy. I didn't even look up at the older man who sat down at the lower table next to mine. I was on task and minding my own business until he dropped a piece of paper. It slid under a chair two tables over. I figured he would have a hard time retrieving it, and I had time for a quick blessing. So, I jumped from my perch and grabbed the paper before he even got to his feet.

"Thank you. What are you working on?" I stared back longing at my computer. "I'm writing a devotion." I lingered there to talk a while praying, "Make me a blessing in this moment." Embracing what could have been seen as an interruption, I realized it was my Right Now Purpose. Jim was a believer. He told me a few of his favorite stories about God's faithfulness in his life. I don't remember our entire conversation, but Jim mentioned he hadn't been to church in years. I told him I had stopped going to church myself, for about seven years. But since I had been back, I realized how much I need it. I need to be fed and encouraged and held accountable on a regular cadence. I need community. He said that made sense. We talked for what seemed like 20 minutes when I said good-bye and returned to my stool. A short time later, after Jim packed up to leave, he stopped at my table and said, "I know God sent you here to talk to me today. Will you please pray with me?"

BAM! This was a Blessing Appointed Moment. I wasn't even set on hanging out in the coffee shop that day. But God put me in the right place at the right time. I was determined to keep my focus, but God was teaching me something. In the same moment, as I pursued my calling—my big dream—God put in front of me a Right Now Purpose in order to display His incredible plan of both/and. I can have big dreams and do small things in the same half hour.

As the assignments get bigger, it's easy to lose sight of our Right Now Purpose. But we need to remember, even big things are really made of many small things. Let's continue to be obedient in the small. Whether you have a big dream or a known calling or even if you are still waiting for God to reveal what lies ahead, He has a good plan to fulfill your Future Promise as you are faithful in your Right Now Purpose.

CHAPTER 7

Share
Meet Spiritual Needs

♪Tell the sweet story of Christ and His love,

Tell of His pow'r to forgive. ♪

Oh, friend, we've been on a journey together. I am so glad you linked arms with me to discover how we execute our one true purpose of bringing glory to God through blessing others. We have learned to concede, plead, intercede, and agree in *Pray*. To *Encourage* with our words, presence, and experience. To *Give* our "such as I have," generously, good, and joyfully. To *Serve* from our bailiwick of blessing, in our big dreams and small things. These selfless acts of blessing plant seeds and develop relationships in order to open the door to the next Blessing Package. *Share*.

Great Commission

"Then Jesus came to them and said, 'All authority in heaven and on earth has been given to me. Therefore go and make disciples of all nations, baptizing them in the name of the Father and of the Son and of the Holy Spirit, and teaching them to obey everything I have commanded you. And surely I am with you always, to the very end of the age," Matthew 28:18-20.

Before leaving earth, Jesus gave this directive, known as the Great Commission, to His followers. His words were for the believers of that day and are an equally relevant command to us today.

There are two distinct categories of people in the world. Every person is either a believer or not. Lost or found. Each individual is destined for eternity in a literal place, heaven or hell. The Great Commission is two-fold; it tells us how we can bless both types of people, saved and unsaved, through sharing. We are commanded to go into the world and preach the gospel to those who do not know Christ and teach those who have accepted Jesus to follow Him more. Be a light to the lost. Build up believers.

Although we are not all called to the full-time vocation of ministry, we are all called to the full-time service of the kingdom. Because I believe my calling is to minister to Christian women, I surmised I was, therefore, not responsible for sharing the gospel with the lost. I thought someone else could bring them in, and I would build them up. As you may have guessed, none of us get a pass on either part of the Great Commission. We are all responsible for both—being a light to the lost and building up believers. While the command to *Share* is not exclusively a *one or the other* scenario, it may inclusively be a *major or minor* situation. Each of us may specialize in sharing with one group or the other, but we will all be given opportunities to be made a blessing to people in both groups.

156

SHARE PART 1:
LIGHT TO THE LOST

In his book, "No Longer a Slumdog," K.P. Yohannan describes the mission work of the organization Gospel for Asia. "It is so important that we do not look at physical assistance as 'fulfilling' the Great Commission. If our goal is simply to improve people's outward status without touching their soul, then we are no different than any of the hundreds of other relief organizations out there."[1]

This truth is the core of being made a blessing. We are not solely called to meet the temporary earthly needs of others through praying, encouraging, giving, and serving. The purpose of loving others is to point them to Jesus. We can feed the hungry, shelter the homeless, and adopt the orphan, while still leaving souls without the knowledge of Christ and the hope of salvation. "What good will it be for someone to gain the whole world, yet forfeit their soul?" Matthew 16:26a.

Through Jesus' sacrificial death on the cross, we as believers enter into restored relationship with God. This unmerited gift, like every other, is a blessing not to hoard, but to give away. The free gift of salvation is given to us so that we may know God and make Him known.

Who Cares?

In Chapter 2 we explored why we keep scrolling when we see problems big and small because, honestly, we don't want to know; we don't want to be bothered. I think it can be the same way with evangelism. Maybe we would rather look the other way because we are content to carry on with our lives. We just keep scrolling so we don't have to think about lost souls.

When I understood I was called to both parts of the Great Commission—be a light to the lost and build up believers—I had to be honest with myself. I gave consideration to other people's eternity exactly zero times per week. I think it's because when we acknowledge there is a problem, we feel compelled to do something about it, and I had no idea what to do about it. My "witnessing" experience was the sum total of missionary dating plus inviting people to church.

1 Timothy 2:4 tells us, God "wants all people to be saved and to come to a knowledge of the truth." It is important to God that His salvation message is spread, and He wants it to be important to us too.

For me, it started with a deep introspective look. Sharing the gospel rarely crossed my mind. Before we share, we have to care. It sounds corny, but it's true. To be effective in sharing the good news we need to genuinely care. Caring isn't as simple as just determining to do so. Authentic concern requires a heart change. So, I began to pray that God would give me a burden for the lost. *Lord, give me a genuine concern for unsaved people.*

Fear

Fear is a real enemy; it keeps us from moving forward in our lives and in blessing. When we share our faith, there is an actual risk of confrontation or rejection. Fear is a normal human response. That is why "Fear not" is one of the most commonly repeated themes in the Bible, because we are prone to do just that.

We aren't alone in being afraid to speak up. When God sent Moses to communicate to the Israelite people, Moses asked God, "What if they do not believe me or listen to me?"[2] I had my own list of questions. "What if sharing my faith causes an argument? Will they think I'm crazy? What if they don't like me anymore? Am I going to say the wrong thing and sound stupid?" All my questions reflected a common underlying concern. "How might I be negatively affected by speaking the truth?" The root of what held me back from witnessing, my fear, was actually cleverly disguised self-focus. We don't need to beat ourselves up for feeling afraid, but we do need to get over ourselves. Fear of sharing the gospel will only be overcome when we become more concerned about the kingdom than our comfort.

"For I am not ashamed of the gospel, because it is the power of God that brings salvation to everyone who believes," Romans 1:16a.

Remember the old-school sitcom "The Brady Bunch?" In one episode, the middle daughter, Jan was nervous about giving a big speech. To help her overcome stage fright, her father suggested, "You picture them sitting there in their underwear."[3] I don't recommend that. It sounds a little creeper-like to me. But the functional principle of this ill-conceived idea is to imagine your audience to be as vulnerable and uncomfortable as you are. They are only human after all.

What if we imagined the true vulnerable state of the human soul? The Bible tells us the impending reality for someone who is not saved is eternity separated from God in a literal hell. The Bible describes the condition of this destination: "the fiery lake of burning sulfur,"[4] "eternal punishment,"[5] "everlasting destruction,"[6] "the blazing furnace, where there will be weeping and gnashing of teeth,"[7] "where the fire never goes out."[8]

I'm not trying to be a downer, but it is imperative for us to view life in perspective of eternity. People we know—our family and friends and coworkers and neighbors—are headed for eternal suffering, and some of us are too bashful to potentially embarrass ourselves by warning them.

"However, I consider my life worth nothing to me; my only aim is to finish the race and complete the task the Lord Jesus has given me—the task of testifying to the good news of God's grace," Acts 20:24. That's it. That is what our redeemed lives are for. To testify about the good news of God's grace. The positions I hold in my circle of influence—

mom, wife, teacher, neighbor, friend—give me the opportunity to fulfill my one true purpose of bringing glory to God by sharing His love with others. Every act of blessing can be a road sign pointing other people to God's grace.

Start Small

Sharing our faith, especially for the first time, can be intimidating. But just like in every other blessing package, we can begin to *Share* by starting small.

My hand shook the first time I wrote a Bible verse in a greeting card. I know it is such a small thing, but it was a big step for me. Post a worship song or sermon quote on social media. Invite someone to church. Even if they refuse, it gets the conversation started. These acts are not in themselves evangelism, but they can be a starting point to get our feet wet in sharing our faith.

I was at a Thirty-One Gifts home party when the consultant explained the company was named for Proverbs 31. I thought, "I love Jesus, and I love bags! I'm in!" When I became a consultant, my message developed over time, but I always opened my parties with something like this: "Thirty-One refers to Proverbs 31, a portion of Scripture that talks about the virtuous woman. She's active in her home, her family, her community, her career, and she still manages to hold it all together and honor God. And that's why I joined Thirty-One. Because Proverbs 31 has been near and dear to my heart as I strive to be the woman God wants me to be." This was a big deal for me. You see, as a trainer at my job, I spoke comfortably in front of hundreds of people about manufacturing topics. But as an adult, I never spoke openly about my faith in front of a group of strangers.

I explained to a Christian friend how Thirty-One was helping me to share. She shrugged, "I don't have any problem sharing my faith." And maybe you don't either, but we don't all just wake up one morning preaching to a stadium. It takes steps to grow, and we have to start somewhere. Don't let inexperience keep you from ever experiencing the opportunity to share God's Word. Simply be obedient; take the next small step. At first, my pre-party monologue was rehearsed. A few times I was asked to repeat the Scripture reference as a guest wrote it down. But one night my party nearly turned into an all-out church service as the ladies asked questions about God, and I was able to lay it all out. I even had the opportunity to pray with one of the guests before the night was over.

Every day, all around us, people are using their platform to share Jesus in big ways and small ways:

Asa's all-time favorite pizza place has John 3:16 printed on their boxes.

My friend Autumn sends daily devotions to a group via text.

The front of a factory on I-75 is lit up with the words "Christ is the Answer."

Our car dealer gives customers a Gideon Bible and an invitation to accept Jesus.

After many years of going my own way, I'm in church today and have a meaningful relationship with Jesus. One of the things that God used to get me there was a concert poster from the band "Third Day" that was hanging in my boss's office. My office was right outside his, so every time I walked by, I caught a glimpse of it. Several times a week during a meeting, I stared directly at the words "Cry Out to Jesus." Over weeks and months, that poster had me thinking. At first, it was, "I like Third Day." Then, "I have their CD somewhere. They used to be my favorite band." Eventually, my thoughts turned to how I hadn't been in church for several years, and maybe it was time to go back. Yes. Hanging a poster in an office is a small thing. But it had eternal impact on my life.

Expanding Your Circle

When we moved 323 miles from the place I had always called home, we had to start over making new connections. Eventually, we discovered a church that felt like home, and I served there on Tuesday nights. We got plugged in with a homeschool group that met on Wednesday. Asa joined a Monday and Thursday night Taekwondo class; it was taught by and mostly attended by Christian families. With church on Sunday, school work and occasional field trips through the week, not to mention all our home projects, our schedule was full.

As I continued to pray to be made a blessing, I considered how to share, and realized my current exposure to the lost was one unsaved neighbor. I had become insulated in a Christian bubble. I didn't do it on purpose. It is normal to gravitate towards people with common interests and places that make us feel comfortable. The fact that I did not personally know anyone I could share the gospel with did not mean there were no unbelievers in my community. Jesus said, "The harvest is plentiful but the workers are few," Matthew 9:37. While becoming isolated in a Christian circle was not intentional, I knew I had to be intentional about expanding my circle of influence.

How does one go about expanding their circle of influence to include more lost people? Here's what I did. Pray. I just began to pray this prayer regularly:

Lord, increase my influence with the lost. Please give me opportunities to share the message of salvation with people who don't know You.

Prayerfully consider your own circle of influence. If you recognize a need to expand your current exposure to unbelievers, I encourage you to pray this too.

It is kind of a scary prayer, though. I had no clue what I was going to do if God actually answered it. As I diligently prayed for Him to expand my circle to include unbelievers, I became aware of many ministries doing evangelical work. My heart tugged to sign up for every one, but I continued to pray. There are many great opportunities, but they are not all my opportunity. God has been faithful to answer my prayer. He has directed me to my own assignments and opened doors for me to share with unsaved people in my community. I have a feeling He's not done yet. God answers when we pray according to His will. Jesus told us, "Ask the Lord of the harvest, therefore, to send workers into his harvest field," Matthew 9:38. We know it is God's will for us to share the good news with the lost, so when we pray for Him to use us in that capacity, He will absolutely answer with our own assignment, hand-picked by Him.

Not to Condemn

"For God did not send his Son into to the world to condemn the world, but to save the world through him," John 3:17.

God didn't send Jesus into the world to condemn the world, and He doesn't send us to condemn the world either. That truth was actually a revelation to me. I honestly thought my job as a Christian was to condemn and criticize anyone who believed differently than me. Our role is to speak the truth in love. I had the truth part down, but I was seriously lacking when it came to love.

In 1 Peter 3:15 we are encouraged to witness "with gentleness and respect." The Bible doesn't tell us directly, but based on his reputation, I wonder if Peter reminded us to defend our faith with "gentleness and respect" because he had to learn the hard way that abrasiveness and disrespect are not effective evangelism tools.

Gentleness and respect are not second nature to me either. During my senior year of high school, I spent every Sunday afternoon at the mall with a group of church friends. One week we stopped at a little shop full of incense and dream catchers. The guy working the register, Tom, was about my age, and I invited him to join us for church. He respectfully declined, explaining he did not believe in God or organized religion. Every Sunday for the rest of the year, I made a point to visit that store and argue with Tom about everything. Politics. Religion. The environment. Whatever social issue was the hot topic for the week. Sometimes it was playful banter, but other times I became downright hostile. I thought if I won the argument, he would have to concede I was right and accept Jesus as his Savior. I honestly believed telling Tom he was wrong and headed for hell was witnessing.

"The kindness of God leads you to repentance."[9] Not pointing out the error of their ways. Not a compelling argument. Kindness. Colossians 4:5-6 says, "Be wise in the way you act toward outsiders; make the most of every opportunity. Let your conversation be always full of grace, seasoned with salt, so that you may know how to answer everyone." I fought so hard to change Tom's mind; Jesus really wanted to change his heart. People do not need us to point out what is wrong with them. They need us to point them to Jesus.

What do I say?

I mentioned a few pages back that inviting people to church is a good small step, a first step. But let's not stop there. Jesus did not tell us to simply invite people to come to church so they could hear the good news. The Great

Commission is to Go. Be the church. Tell people the good news.

When it comes down to the practical application of sharing the gospel one real reason that may hold us back is simply not feeling like we have the right words to speak. Not knowing what to say can keeps us from saying anything at all. It's a real obstacle, but one we can overcome. God loves every person so much, He sent His only Son Jesus to die for them. He wants them to know it. He wants us to tell them. As we consider what to say, keep these truths in mind: It is not our job to convince; it is the Holy Spirit's job to convict. We are called to obedience; God is responsible for the outcome.

Your Heart Speaks

A misconception about sharing is we must have a plan, a formula, say all the right words. Witnessing is about starting a conversation, sharing from the heart. People are hip to a sales pitch. *Share* won't be effective if the dialogue is contrived. As we build relationships, God will show us opportunities to incorporate His message into the conversation. It has to happen organically. We can lead the discussion, but not force it.

You wouldn't have to talk to me long to know I'm Asa's mom and Chris's wife. What we love naturally flows out of us. When people love their sports team, even a losing team, they slap on a bumper sticker, wear the T-shirt, get a tattoo.

Kombucha rocked my world a few years ago. Every person I encountered in the following months was offered a swig. (If you're not familiar, kombucha is fermented sweet tea with a culture of yeast and bacteria. Yum!) I plastered pics of my growing colony on Facebook. I told anybody who would listen about Kombucha's many health benefits—Probiotics! Antioxidants! Why? It's the mouth-heart connection we talked about in chapter 3. The mouth speaks what the heart is full of. When we are totally into something, it just comes out. Naturally. Our brains incorporate it into conversation without trying. I never second guessed myself. "Should I tell them about my drink? What if they're offended? What if they don't like probiotics?" It just came up in conversation. Especially if I had recently enjoyed a refreshing drink, if it was fresh on my mind.

Jesus, in comparison to kombucha, has done significantly more for me. More is at stake than digestive health. It's eternity. So why in the world am I reluctant to share what God has done for me and offer others a drink of living water? If I have experienced Jesus' new mercy today, it's fresh on my mind; I want to talk about it. His love will flow out naturally in conversation if we don't inhibit it.

"Neither do people light a lamp and put it under a bowl. Instead they put it on its stand, and it gives light to everyone in the house," Matthew 5:15.

Your Story Speaks

In John chapter 4 we read the story of a Samaritan woman who went to draw water from a well and had a life-altering encounter with Jesus. So taken by their conversation, she left her water jar behind and went back to her town to tell all the people about Jesus. "Many of the Samaritans from that town believed in him because of the woman's testimony."[10]

I'm not good at giving impromptu answers to difficult questions. Jesus turned my life right-side-up. But I was completely caught off guard when a woman at church asked, "Have you shared your personal testimony?" I had not, and honestly, I needed more than just a moment to gather my thoughts. In order to articulate what Jesus had done in my life, I had to take time to process my own story. I spent the next several months thinking over the previous 40 years, trying to remember my faith journey, where I had been and how far God had brought me.

"Always be prepared to give an answer to everyone who asks you to give a reason for the hope that you have," 1 Peter 3:15b. The passage doesn't say we have to have all the answers. It says to give a reason for the hope that *you* have. That's your personal story. Why you accepted Jesus as your Savior. How your life changed since making Him your Lord. We each have a unique testimony of God's grace in our lives. Knowing your own story and being able to articulate it provides an answer for your hope.

God's Word Speaks

After Jesus' encounter with the woman at the well, the Samaritans urged Him to stay with them. "And because of his words, many more came to believe."[11]

God's Word speaks for itself. The entire Bible is the story of God's great love and pursuit of humanity, to save us from our sin and bring about redemption. Because of His Word, many will believe.

In the past, my job was to teach boring, technical, manufacturing classes, including electro-static discharge (basically, static electricity). Science is not my forte. I didn't know much about the matter, and I wasn't interested enough to make an effort to learn. I had a good outline and was able to memorize an engaging presentation, so the class went smoothly. Until the end. When people started asking questions. At that point, I lost my credibility because I didn't understand the subject; I simply regurgitated information. The only answers I had were in the presentation, the person who created it had retired, so I didn't even know where to get answers.

Teaching ergonomics was completely different for me. Long before conducting the class, I attended weeks of intense training and spent many months of putting the principles into practice. I had practical application not just theoretical knowledge of ergonomics. I was by no means an expert, but I had enough understanding of the material to teach it well. When questions would arise, I was able to answer many from my training. When I was not sure of the answer, instead of saying, "I don't know," I was able to respond, "I'm not sure, but I know where to get an answer." My training included a reference manual and the phone number of an ergonomist who was happy to answer my questions.

Reciting God's Word is not the same as knowing it. We don't have to be Bible scholars and memorize the entire New Testament. But if we go around spouting concepts we don't understand, someone will eventually call our bluff and ask a question. Where does that leave us? Back at square one, where we keep quiet because we don't know what to say? No. It means we start with what we know, but we must be willing to study to learn more.

John 3:16 is the first verse most of us memorize. "For God so loved the world that he gave his one and only Son, that whoever believes in him shall not perish but have eternal life." This verse is a summary of the entire gospel message in a single sentence. If you know and understand this verse, you know the good news of God's Word.

The five verses I shared as an invitation in Chapter 2 are known as the Romans Road. I like this tool because it's the salvation story contained in one book of the Bible. It spells everything out in detail and gives a lot of talking points. Stay immersed in God's Word. Knowing what Scripture says is key to our own personal understanding and communication of the Bible. Rather than memorizing passages that don't make sense to you, find verses in the Bible that speak to your heart and your story. Verses you understand and can in turn communicate.

The Spirit Speaks

In Mark 13:11b Jesus tells His followers, "Do not worry beforehand about what to say. Just say whatever is given you at the time, for it is not you speaking, but the Holy Spirit." We see in Mark 13:3, Peter was sitting on the Mount of Olives with Jesus when He said don't worry about what to say. But later we know Peter said, "Always be prepared to give an answer to everyone." And Paul said, "Know how to answer everyone." Are these commands contradictory? Not at all.

We can do our part in being prepared to give an answer by processing our story so we can share it and by knowing what God's Word says. There is no magic formula. Each encounter sharing the gospel will be different because each person is unique. Some will be moved by the love of God that flows naturally from us, others will respond to our personal testimony or by the witness of God's Word. We don't know what another person needs to hear, but God does. Being empty of ourselves and full of the Spirit will allow us to hear His voice when the time comes.

I didn't know why Tiffany was at my house that evening. I pulled a few more weeds and headed into the garage where she was sitting all alone. I made some small talk about school and work and her boyfriend. She started rambling on about how they had recently broken up for the 87th time and how badly he had been treating her. Yet she was determined to "hang out" with him, desperate to "still be friends." I blurted out, "Don't you know your worth?" Tiffany retorted, "Oh sure! As soon as I changed my status to 'single' there were a ton of hot guys begging for a date." I shook my head slowly. "No. I mean that you were made in the image of God! You are worth far more than the number of guys asking you out. Most of us spend our lives looking for our value or trying to fill our void with the wrong things. For some it's relationships or career, others look to drugs or alcohol. But we will only find

169

our true value in God, the One who created us. He loved you so much that He sent His only Son Jesus to die for you."

Witnessing to Tiffany was not on my agenda for that day. Honestly, we'd never had more than a totally surface conversation, and it never even occurred to me to share the gospel with her. In fact, our exchange took me completely off guard. I was surprised myself by the words that came out of my mouth. But the Holy Spirit gave me words to speak. I'm not saying some weird supernatural thing happened where my mouth was overtaken, and I had no control over the words I was speaking. I formed each word, I spoke with my own mouth, the words I used were my own vocabulary. But I did not worry about what to say; the words flowed from my lips naturally. The Holy Spirit led me to say just the right thing. Later, I thought back to the words I had spoken, "Hey, that was spot on! Perfectly put!" And that's how I knew it was the Holy Spirit through me and not words contrived on my own.

Do not be afraid! God will equip you for the task. He will not leave you helpless, unable to execute His plan. But He does expect participation on our part. We do have to keep our hearts prepared by staying in constant communication with Him and being diligent about studying His Word.

Lord, I trust You to equip me for the call of spreading the gospel. I pray what Paul said in Ephesians 6:19b, "That whenever I speak, words may be given me so that I will fearlessly make known the mystery of the gospel."

Your Actions Speak

"Wives, in the same way submit yourselves to your own husbands so that, if any of them do not believe the word, they may be won over without words by the behavior of their wives, when they see the purity and reverence of your lives," 1 Peter 3:1-2.

170

Sometimes we don't need to speak at all. Other people may be won over without words, by our behavior. That's great news! Why didn't I lead with that? We all have people in our lives who cannot receive the truth from us. Maybe it's because they know us too well; they know our past; they've seen our shortcomings. They wonder if the change will stick or doubt we have really changed at all. There's no use trying to convince them. Explanation is less effective than demonstration.

Our best witness is our walk. That is a relief, but it is also a challenge. It means our lives really need to do the talking. Actions are more credible than words. By no means are we expected to be perfect. But we need to continually grow to be more like Jesus so other people can see Him reflected in our lives.

Father God, we both know I'm not perfect. I'm grateful You don't expect me to be. Help me to live a holy life. Show me areas where I need to be more like Jesus, so others will see Christ through me.

What's Your Number?

My heart fluttered at the thought of typing the word "witnessing." Truth is, as I approached writing *Share*, I flashed back to a sticky August evening when I was middle school aged. I squirmed in a metal folding chair under a big tent. On the stage was a white-haired preacher in a three-piece suit; his polyester tie pushed snugly into his Adam's apple. Sweat dripped from his brow as he jumped up and down behind the pulpit spitting words. "What's your number?!" He spouted off some triple-digit number of the people he had "won to the Lord" and grilled the audience for their numbers. My heart pounded, reverberating in my eardrums, drowning out the rest of his two-hour hellfire and damnation sermon. I didn't have a number. I still don't have a number. I know now that none of us have a number.

God does not sponsor a soul-winner's scoreboard. In fact, keeping score is closely related to taking credit. Striving for a number is the result of pride. Not one of us is personally credited with anyone else's salvation. Paul explained this truth:

"I planted the seed, Apollos watered it, but God has been making it grow. So neither the one who plants nor the one who waters is anything, but only God, who makes things grow," 1 Corinthians 3:6-7.

Our gracious Father often gives us the opportunity to participate in His Blessing Cycle by sharing the truth of salvation with others. But God does the real work; He gets all the credit. Jesus confirmed it. "No one can come to me unless the Father who sent me draws them," John 6:44a.

Our motivation in sharing cannot be to keep score hoping to earn something from God. The Great Commission is not about a badge on our sash when we get to heaven. The reason we share is to fulfill our one true purpose of bringing glory to God. We don't get the credit. The good news is, we also don't bear the responsibility. We are called to obedience; God handles the outcome.

A couple of years ago, I produced a short devotional booklet and felt led to share the Roman's Road in the center. My friend Trina sent me this message. "My father-in-law is in the hospital dying of cancer. My husband wanted to share the gospel with him and didn't know how to do it. I picked up your book, opened it, took it to him and said, 'Here you go.' My father-in-law accepted Jesus and said the weight of the world is off his shoulders. Amen! He even asked to share it with his wife."

I am not telling you this story in any way to boast or to take credit for what God did for Trina's father-in-law. When I received her message, I cried for days, humbled that God

172

would see fit to allow me to participate. I didn't prepare the ground or plant the seed or water it or harvest it. But God graciously allowed me to have a small part in this man's redemption story by typing a few words on a page. Trina played a small part in her loved one accepting Jesus, and so did her husband Scott. It is likely, over his many years, others had planted seeds as well. But the Holy Spirit is the One who did the work in this man's heart and drew him to Jesus. Praise God! He gets all the credit.

Home

We have the responsibility and the privilege to share the message of salvation with our own children. "Start children off on the way they should go, and even when they are old they will not turn from it," Proverbs 22:6. Each child is an individual human being with free will. We cannot force them to accept the truth, but we have great influence in their lives. It is not enough to take our kids to Sunday School and hope they pay attention. Through heart-to-heart conversations, we can do our part to ensure our kids have a clear understanding of their need for a Savior and how to accept Jesus.

I will never forget standing next to my son at the kitchen counter as he prayed to accept Jesus as his Savior. Nothing in my life compares to that moment.

Grandpa Red

I wish you could've known Grandpa Red. He was my hero. The kind of man the world hasn't seen since the era of the John Wayne movie. He was a hard-working, tough-as-nails man who had a soft spot for his grandkids. Well into my adulthood, I sat wide-eyed at Grandpa's feet as he spun tales of coonhounds and shotguns, of fishing poles and pick-up trucks. It was my 28th birthday, this time I sat, not at his feet, but leaning on the cold metal rail of his hospital bed, still enchanted by his stories of adventure. I was angry at first because my husband was unable to take me to the hospital. I didn't want to go alone, but God in His sovereignty knew I needed these few undivided moments, just Grandpa and me. I reasoned he would be fine. Grandpa Red was nothing if not a fighter; he had real battle wounds to prove it. Surely cancer was no match for this titan. But as weeks passed and diagnoses were communicated, it became clear, time was short. I could not shake the fear of losing him on earth, far worse, the fear of losing him for eternity. How could I go on not knowing if I would ever see Grandpa Red again?

We rarely talked much about deep things like death or the reality of life after this one on earth. Our conversations were always light and full of laughter. I knew it would be incredibly awkward, but I also knew I would never forgive myself if my grandpa left this life, and I had not personally shared the truth of the gospel with him. I had no idea how to begin. There was so much to say. I poured out my heart through pencil on paper. My dad stood at my side in the spare bedroom of my grandparents' home—the room where I had spent so many summer nights sleeping over. The twin beds had been moved out to make way for a cold hospital bed. Trembling, I choked out handwritten words of the tear-stained letter. I recounted some of my favorite memories: A fist-full of Sweet William's Grandpa brought me one Spring day; he bent down and whispered not to tell Grandma Phyllis he'd stolen them from her garden. The Lake Erie spray in my face as we sped along in his little fishing boat. I told Grandpa Red I longed so much to know I would see him again after our lives were through, and we can choose eternity in heaven with Jesus. Grandpa's eyes were closed; he was fighting to breathe that afternoon. I'm not sure if he was able to hear the words I said through his own gasps.

I don't know what effect my words had on Grandpa. The hard truth is, we cannot impose a decision; we can only share the options. I do know Grandpa Red prayed a prayer of salvation with a preacher friend of the family before he took his final breath on this earth. I have real hope we will be reunited someday.

It is terribly difficult to watch anyone suffer, especially someone you love fiercely. Imagine the immeasurably worse suffering a loved one will endure if they spend eternity in the torment of hell. None of us is promised another day. Not everyone sees their end coming clearly like my grandfather did when a doctor enumerated the days he had left. My heart is to share with the people I love before it's too late, not to wait until the perceived end to communicate the truth.

SHARE PART 2: BUILD UP BELIEVERS

We've explored the first part of the Great Commission, be a light to the lost, but we aren't done yet. The second part tells us how to bless our brothers and sisters in Christ through sharing. Building up believers involves promoting their spiritual growth and well-being.

Example

I met Christie at a women's conference, and we became fast friends. As weeks and months progressed, our relationship took an odd turn. I heard Christie repeating phrases and verses I quoted. She downloaded every song on my playlist, reposted half of my Facebook page, followed all the same people on Twitter, and bought each book I mentioned reading. Christie was copy-cat-ing me. At first, I was a little weirded out. Did I have a stalker? Not really, Christie was just following my lead as she figured out what it looks like to live life as a believer. As she grew in her relationship with Jesus, Christie began to find her own rhythms in walking out her faith.

Our urge is to tell people, "Don't follow me; follow Jesus." It is true, our commission is to make disciples of Jesus, not disciples of ourselves. But Paul said, "Follow my example, as I follow the example of Christ," 1 Corinthians 11:1. You see, people are watching us whether we like it or not. The challenge for us is to live a life worthy of being imitated. We can be a blessing to others by pointing them to Jesus through the way we represent Him. The truth applies: Our best witness is our walk.

Yes, we are human, and we will not get it right 100% of the time. That's good news for other humans who will also stumble occasionally. In 1 Timothy 4:12b, Paul instructed Timothy to "set an example for the believers in speech, in conduct, in love, in faith and in purity." What an ambitious list. Our goal is not perfection, but to lead by example, model what it means to be a Christ-follower.

Discipleship

Introducing someone to Jesus makes a convert, what we do next is help them to become a disciple. A disciple is a learner, a true Christ follower. Knowing how to follow Jesus is not automatic for a new believer. When a newborn baby is brought into the kingdom, we cannot leave them to fend for themselves. They need nurturing to grow. Spiritual maturity is not directly related to the length of time someone has been a Christian. We all develop at different rates and in different areas of our lives. Discipleship is helping a newer or less mature believer progressively navigate the basics of becoming a follower of Jesus.

One of the great joys of parenting has been seeing my son discover new things for the first time, especially in those early years. When I asked, "Where's your nose?" My toddler smiled, placed his pointer finger squarely on the tip of his nose. We burst out in laughter and clapping. "Yay! There's your nose!" The game went on for hours. We couldn't wait to show Grandma on our next visit. "Asa, show Grandma! Where's your nose?" Grandma didn't shake her head and say, "Everybody knows where your nose is." She celebrated right along with us. I didn't say, "I'm the one who taught him where his nose is." I didn't have to make it about me. I let my little boy have his moment.

I experienced that same type of joy when I had the opportunity to help someone navigate the Bible for the first time. I pointed out the Old and New Testaments, showed her the table of contents to help locate books of the Bible, and explained how chapters and verses are broken down. I was awestruck in that moment. I had been in church all my life and learned those things so long ago, they were literally second nature to me. As I saw other people walking around in adult bodies, it was easy to assume they should know the things I know. I forgot baby Christians come in all shapes and sizes and ages and demographics. I didn't even grasp until that moment that simply opening the Bible and finding a verse for the first time could be such a discovery. I don't ever want to lose the wonder of helping someone take baby steps in their faith. Of course, it is nothing I take credit for, but what a blessing that God would allow me to participate in pointing people to deeper relationship with Himself.

In Luke 13:6-9, Jesus tells the parable of a man who had a fig tree growing in his vineyard. For three years he had looked for fruit to grow on the tree and was disappointed with the result. He told the vineyard caretaker, "Cut it down! Why should it use up the soil?" But the worker insisted, "Leave it alone for one more year, and I'll dig around it and fertilize it." Growing a tree is an investment of time and energy; there is much work and nurturing involved.

In the same way, growing a disciple requires an investment of time and energy. We cannot force people to grow, but we can help make the conditions right by providing them with the resources, care, and attention they need to flourish. Discipleship is a relational process of imparting spiritual knowledge. Whether in a group or one on one, the goal is to equip believers. We do this by helping others develop spiritual disciplines essential for growth: prayer, Bible study, gathering in community. We promote maturity by encouraging and facilitating a person's next steps in their walk with Christ, like baptism and serving.

Sometimes even with all the right conditions, a plant or a person simply doesn't grow. It can be disappointing when we have invested our time and energy, but we are responsible for obedience, not the outcome.

Mentoring

Discipleship is geared toward leading and teaching newer or less mature believers in the basics of Christianity. Mentoring is more intimately relational, coming alongside, linking arms with another believer. A mentoring relationship can be beneficial to believers at any stage. While mentoring is not specifically mentioned in the Bible, from Moses and Joshua to Paul and Timothy, Scripture highlights the value of mentoring relationships.

I was excited for Ladies' Night Out at church; it was kind of a big deal to put on makeup and clothes with no paint splotches or food stains. Dianne complimented my scarf as I walked by, so I paused at her table to talk. Soon I was sitting, and before we knew it, an hour had passed. Dianne and I attended the same Bible study on Wednesday nights. We had exchanged pleasantries in the past but never had a real conversation. The book I was reading at the time encouraged me to find an accountability partner, someone to pray for the journey and encourage me to stay on track. During our conversation, I felt prompted to ask Dianne if she'd be willing. By the end of the night, we decided to make it official and signed up for our church's mentoring program. It's funny the way God makes things happen. I had invited at least five different friends to join me that evening, several declined. I was disappointed when the only one who said "Yes" stood me up at the last minute. I wasn't expecting to show up alone, but if any of my friends had come with me, I would have been preoccupied with them. Because I was solo, I was able to engage in this conversation with Dianne that I am certain was a divine appointment.

"Because we loved you so much, we were delighted to share with you not only the gospel of God but our lives as well," 1 Thessalonians 2:8b. Mentoring means being a blessing by cultivating a deep, meaningful, spiritual relationship.

A mentor provides support and accountability. She encourages a mentee, builds her up, and propels her forward. Unlike a life coach, a mentor does not tell a mentee what to think, what to do, or how to do it. A good mentor comes alongside another person to help guide and empower them to lean on God for direction. You see, although she often gives wise counsel, her thoughts and experiences are secondary to biblical wisdom. Dianne doesn't offer her opinion or sage advice when I face a decision. She helps me process the facts, then points me to God's Word and the leading of the Holy Spirit.

The mentoring program we participated in was a commitment to meet a couple of times a month for six months. Mentoring does not have to be a formal relationship with set parameters. In fact, in some cases, it happens so organically, it doesn't need a label. I haven't seen Dianne in person since I moved years ago, but we keep in touch through technology, and she continues to be a mentor to me from across the miles.

Dianne has been instrumental in my spiritual growth, and she has also been an indispensable part of *Make Me a Blessing*. When I got serious about writing this book, my mentor agreed to take on the role of editor, and God has used her to impact this project in a powerful way. She has a tremendous command of the English language and always catches my silly mistakes. But I know I can depend on her for something far more important than checking the grammar and mechanics of my writing. I trust Dianne's understanding of Scripture and know she will hold me accountable to sound doctrine. Her encouragement, positive reinforcement, and candid feedback have kept me going when I wanted to give up.

Genesis 12:3a reiterates the Blessing Cycle. "I will bless those who bless you." I know I could not possibly repay Dianne's kindness to me, but I believe God's promises are true. I have been blessed so abundantly by my friend, Dianne, and I pray regularly for our loving Father to bless her in return.

Home

Because our circle of influence begins in the home, there is no more important place to bless through sharing. The same principles apply—leading by example, modeling Christianity, and teaching basic disciplines to promote growth. But because we have a different, more intimate relationship with our immediate family, Scripture gives a few specifics on blessing our own people.

"These commandments that I give you today are to be on your hearts. Impress them on your children. Talk about them when you sit at home and when you walk along the road, when you lie down and when you get up. Tie them as symbols on your hands and bind them on your foreheads. Write them on the doorframes of your houses and on your gates," Deuteronomy 6:6-9.

The single most important thing we can teach our children—more important than any life skill or discipline—is God's Word. This passage in Deuteronomy points us to more than a one-time conversation, but a lifestyle of biblical truth. Keeping God's Word in our own hearts, talking about it, making Scripture visible in our homes. In this way, we bless our families; we build them up by keeping God's Word at the center of our lives.

We cannot chart the course for our children's futures, but we can point them in the right direction. "Bring them up in the training and instruction of the Lord," Ephesians 6:4b. Through training and instruction in God's Word, we can point them to Jesus.

Men and women are different. Even with the best intentions to bless my husband, I don't always build him up the way he needs, because I default to duplicating my needs. Scripture gives us a clear understanding of the best way to build up our spouse. "However, each one of you must love his wife as he loves himself, and the wife must respect her husband," Ephesians 5:33. I need love; my husband needs respect. I bless him best by reaching his heart in the way God designed him.

Community

"Now you are the body of Christ, and each one of you is part of it," 1 Corinthians 12:27.

We are parts of a whole; we need each other. The body of Christ cannot fully function apart. God designed us for relationship with Himself and with each other. We are better together. Church attendance is a vital part of Christian community, but there's more. The purpose is to cultivate deep spiritual relationships, to do this Christ-following life together.

Community happens in many forms. It is not determined by the number of people or the location of meeting. I've been in groups of as many as 50, as few as four, and have experienced community in individual relationships. We've met in churches and libraries, in homes and coffee shops and fire stations. Four characteristics set authentic Christian community apart from other friend groups; it is distinguished by:

Christ. Connection. Contribution. Commitment.

Christ: If Jesus is not the reason we gather, our group is just a book club or a coffee crew. We need those too. But authentic Christian community is for the purpose of spiritual development. Some groups do deep-dive Bible studies and others are more about fellowship. No matter the format or curriculum, Christ must be the center of all our activities in community.

Connection: Growing together is an essential outcome of community. We grow closer to God and closer to each other. Putting on artificial religiousness inhibits our growth and prevents us from letting others in. We have to take off our masks, break down our walls. Fueled by honesty and transparency, authentic community creates a safe place to be seen and known, to connect and belong.

Contribution: Thriving community requires participation. We don't have to be the leader to play a vital role in our groups. When we share what the Holy Spirit is speaking to us and how God is working in our lives, others will be blessed by our contribution.

We can't approach community with self-focus. Gathering is not exclusively about being fed or having a place to express ourselves; it is not all about what we get out of it. We each have a purpose, a mission, a contribution. "That is, that you and I may be mutually encouraged by each other's faith," Romans 1:12. Mutual encouragement includes intentional contribution as well as active listening. That means I'm not too busy formulating my response to hear what others have to say. We gather together to participate in the Blessing Cycle— to encourage and to be encouraged.

Commitment: Surface level commitment produces surface level relationships. Hebrews 10:25a says, "Not giving up meeting together, as some are in the habit of doing, but encouraging one another." We make time for what is important to us. Real life happens, family emergencies and illness occasionally cause us to miss gathering. But, sometimes I just don't feel like being around people, or I don't like the study they picked. I need to be reminded, it's not all about me. Community means we show up. If we want to grow, if we want to bless our brothers and sisters in Christ through sharing, we must make meeting together a priority. We are blessed when others show up and participate. The Blessing Cycle is completed, we bless them in return, by being committed to community.

One particular group shaped me like no other. God ordained an intimate weekly gathering of like-minded, Jesus-loving women. We prayed. We studied God's Word. We did life together. During that season connecting with these women, I experienced the greatest spiritual growth of my life. We were equally engaged in our group dynamic and our individual relationships. No one pretended to be more spiritual than the others. Everyone showed up. Everyone participated. Everyone shared. Everyone grew. Everyone was blessed. Everyone was a blessing.

"As iron sharpens iron, so one person sharpens another," Proverbs 27:17.

When we moved a couple of years ago, I had to leave behind that amazing group of Jesus-loving women who had become such an important part of my heart and my life. Our move was unorthodox and drawn out. We lived on a remote chunk of land and spent every moment traveling or preparing our fixer-upper for the impending winter. It was difficult for me to make new connections. I spent the most part of six months alone with my husband and son. During that season, I desperately missed my friends; I struggled with loneliness and understanding God's plan.

That difficult time had a purpose. God was teaching me, molding me. He had abundantly blessed me with the gift of community. Although it was lonely, I believe God also blessed me with the lack of community for a season. During that time, I was reminded what it feels like to be alone, not only so I would appreciate fellowship as a blessing, but so I would also recognize that the women around me need connection. Since then, God has given me many opportunities to help meet that need. Just like every other blessing in my life, God blessed me with community, not for my benefit alone, but so that I would bless others. Every one of us needs a place to connect and belong. We need Jesus, and we need each other. We were made for community.

CHAPTER 8

Inspire
Compel Others to Meet Needs

As our time together draws to a close, my hope is that we have gone past the fad-diet stage and have made blessing a lifestyle. We know it takes six weeks or 40 days to create a habit. If you are reading this book, one chapter per week, as part of a small group study, you should have a firmly developed pattern as we enter into week eight of this journey. If you have read the book in a shorter time, keep going until blessing has become a regular part of your daily life. I pray we all get to the place where blessing is instinctive; it's second nature. At the end of most days, I reflect back, wondering if I have been a blessing. I am continually in awe of God's goodness to allow me to participate in His Blessing Cycle. Especially when instances come to mind that I didn't even process as blessing while I was just instinctively doing them. I know you'll be just as blessed when you find the same thing to be true for you.

We've come a long way together, but we are not quite done. The mission doesn't end with having established our own daily habit of asking God to make us a blessing and being obedient in the opportunities He gives us. The final way we can be made a blessing is to *Inspire*, to compel others to meet needs, to execute their one true purpose of bringing glory to God by being a blessing.

All People?

Immediately after making the promise in our key verse, "I will bless you....so that you will be a blessing," God takes it one step further. He tells Abraham, "**All peoples** on earth will be blessed through you," Genesis 12:3b *(emphasis mine)*. Abraham didn't even hesitate. The very next verse says, "So Abraham went." I want to grow to respond to God that way. He speaks; so I go. My typical reply is to question everything. *Seriously? How? How could I possibly bless all people? You know I'm only one person, right? When exactly is this going to happen? I'm not getting any younger.*

Check out this New Testament parallel of God's promise to Abraham. In Matthew 28:19a Jesus commissions his followers, "Therefore go and make disciples of **all nations**," *(emphasis mine).* Again, I would have a few questions. *All nations? You mean everyone? How is that going to work?*

We were each born at an appointed time, in an appointed place, with an appointed role in history. Our circle of influence is finite—we cannot personally reach every human being on the planet. But the good news is, where our circle ends, someone else's circle begins. We can't do it alone; we were never meant to bless all people all on our own. We are each called to meet a specific set of needs within our reach. Then, through our actions, we can motivate others to choose their own assignments in meeting needs.

You see, *Inspire* goes beyond that warm feeling you get after watching a Hallmark movie. More than evoking positive emotions, inspiration is dynamic, a catalyst, a stimulant to movement. Inspiration is love's call to action, recruiting partners in perpetuating the Blessing Cycle.

When I consider the movement created by blessing, I envision a revolver. One motion lifts a bullet up into the chamber and another propels it forward out of the barrel. My son's Pez dispenser collection works in much the same way. The candy is pulled up into position and pushed ahead to be used. Through every other blessing package, we have been lifting people in an upward motion. *Inspire* is a force, creating forward momentum. Propelling others into the good works of the kingdom of God.

"I alone cannot change the world, but I can cast a stone across the waters to create many ripples." –Mother Teresa[1]

If we bless the people within our circle of influence and they are compelled to bless those around them, we create a ripple of blessing. As blessing is inspired to the third and fourth and fifth generation, more stones are cast, more ripples are created. The potential reach is limitless—all peoples, all nations, blessing and being blessed.

Hebrews 10:24 says, "And let us consider how we may spur one another on toward love and good deeds." In this verse, Paul defines *Inspire*. We are on the last leg of our journey together; last but certainly not least. Inspire is not a footnote or addendum. As we have grown in learning to be made a blessing ourselves, the next logical and necessary step is to bless others by engaging them in the Blessing Cycle. Blessing is incomplete until we spur one another on toward love and good deeds. Let's dig in together and discover how each of us can inspire, propel others forward in fulfilling their own call to be a blessing.

Lord, I know that my circle of influence is finite. I cannot reach everyone, but teach me to inspire those around me, creating a limitless ripple of blessing.

There are four ways to inspire others to bless:

Example. Express. Engage. Empower.

Example

"In the same way, let your light shine before others, that they may see your good deeds and glorify your Father in heaven," Matthew 5:16.

We spent ample time in the last chapter talking about being a living example. By engaging in the lifestyle of *Make Me a Blessing*, people will observe our actions and be inspired to follow.

Inspiring by example is subtle. Often, neither the person being inspired nor the person being an inspiration realizes what is happening. My Grandma Phyllis was the consummate hostess with a true servant's heart. A person could hardly leave her home without being served a home-cooked meal complete with seconds, dessert, and a take-home box. Grandma never explained her service to me. I don't think she realized she was blessing others; serving was just something she did naturally. I must have picked up on her example. Food is my love language. If you walk through the front door of my little log cabin on the creek, expect to be offered a cold drink and a bite to eat. I did not learn this in a conscious effort to follow my grandma's lead. Her selfless acts of service simply rubbed off on me.

One random act of kindness had such a ripple effect, it made our local 6 o'clock news. A drive-thru customer paid for the person in the car behind them. The driver whose meal was purchased paid for the following car. That person paid for the next in line, and the person after them paid for the one after. By the time the restaurant closed that night, an unbroken cycle of 167 customers had reportedly paid for the meal of the person in the car behind them.

I ducked into my favorite coffee shop, Sabaidee, hoping a mid-day cup of pick-me-up would stave off the December chill. Mesmerized by the crafting of frothy delight, I barely noticed the weeping girl standing next to me. She poured out her heart to the barista who paused mid-foam to look at me and say, "Are you in a hurry?" "Not at all." I was, in fact, not eager to get home and begin climbing the awaiting mountain of laundry. The barista replied, "I'm going to pray with this girl quick." She used the edge of her apron to wipe her hands before laying them on the young lady. Employees and even a few other customers gathered 'round as this girl was lifted in prayer. This gift moment from God, the blessing I observed and was privileged to participate in, would later bless me with inspiration.

An unexpected package arrived December 26. I traded the mail carrier for a hand-made ornament wrapped in cellophane. Her eyes pooled to the rim just before spilling over, her heart still tender from the passing of a dear friend. "I'll pray for you," I replied. She attempted a smile and walked away as the screen door squeaked to a slam. Before she made it off the porch, I startled her by bounding out the door hollering, "Wait! Let's pray right now." BAM! I didn't know it at the time, but my visit to the coffee shop a few days earlier was a Blessing Appointed Moment. Not an opportunity for me to bless, but an appointment for me to observe blessing in action and later be inspired to bless in a similar way. That moment has continued to inspire me to change my approach to prayer. More and more, my response has been "Let's pray right now," instead of "I'll pray for you later." Whenever possible, I want to bless others by stopping in the moment and agreeing together in prayer.

Express

Grandma Phyllis inspired me with more than her example. She used her words to urge others to bless. When I was a little girl, Grandma patted the cushion next to her on the floral brocade couch, and I plopped down by her side as she read her poetry aloud. Some poems had me giggling or chiming along with the refrain, but others were her heart poured out on a page. Grandma's voice wavered, and her eyes welled with tears, but honestly, I just didn't get it. *I get it now, Grandma.*

One Mother's Day, a poem about her mother was printed in the local newspaper. Besides that, Grandma's writing never met eyes outside of our family and her friends. Until now. She is in heaven with Jesus, and I wonder if she knows she's officially being "published." Of course, I am certain of this one thing—in this moment, she is surrounded with far greater joy than any earthly recognition could ever bring. I am humbled and honored to share Grandma Phyllis's inspirational call to bless:

Do Something Nice for Someone Today

by Phyllis Ann Correll

To make someone happy or make a new friend
With just a nice smile or a wave of your hand
You can't go through life with your eyes closed tight
Put on a face that's happy and bright
Show everybody you really care
Help one another and please try to share
Some are downtrodden and have lost their way
Above all else teach them to pray
Do something nice for someone today

Asa tossed his backpack into the trunk of the car. As soon as the passenger door slammed shut, before his seatbelt clicked, I began telling him about my opportunity to bless that afternoon. A scruffy, weathered man stood outside of the grocery store rubbing his hands together, occasionally cupping them next to his mouth to breathe deeply between. His mismatched gloves were worn thin with several missing fingertips. "Do you need some warm gloves?" Asa and I had assembled blessing bags a few months earlier, preparing for just such an encounter. I was thrilled to finally be giving one away. My son replied, "Should you be telling me this? Isn't it bragging?" Good point, Asa. I explained that as his parent, it is my responsibility to set an example of blessing. Since he is not always with me to observe my actions, I need to communicate how God uses me to bless. If I did not tell him, he would not know it was happening and may not understand the importance. I let him know that because of our relationship, sometimes I tell him more personal things, details that I would not necessarily share as much with other people. The purpose is to bring glory to God, by demonstrating ways we can be a blessing. But I did make sure he knows he's right; we don't go around bragging about our good deeds.

It is possible to discretely explain our blessing opportunities to others, not to draw attention to ourselves, but to inspire our brothers and sisters to be a blessing. In Ephesians 4:29b, Paul instructs us to speak "only what is helpful for building others up according to their needs, that it may benefit those who listen." The key to inspiring instead of bragging is to consider how our words will build up and benefit the person hearing. We can learn from each other's experiences. Blessing is not intuitive to everyone. Some may be eager to bless but need a little further instruction on what the practical application looks like. The emphasis must not be how good we are to bless, but God's goodness in allowing His children to participate in His plan.

The purpose in writing my story of *Make Me a Blessing* is not at all to brag, not simply to entertain, and not solely to disseminate information. In expressing the truth that our ordinary lives can have eternal impact because we are blessed to be a blessing, my hope is that you will be inspired to bless. That we would each take on the mission to fulfill our one true purpose of bringing glory to God by blessing others.

Now it's your turn to share your own story of being blessed and being made a blessing. How has this message impacted you? Compel others to bless by sharing the principles you've seen at work in your own life and in the lives of those around you. Give a real-life testimony of the Blessing Cycle in action. Check out the last few pages of this book to connect with me and to find free resources to help you communicate the message of *Make Me a Blessing*. Recommend the book; give a copy to a friend; invite your small group to study this together. Get people engaged in the mission of blessing by spreading the word.

When children are quite young, barely able to form complete sentences, adults are already asking the question. "What do you want to be when you grow up?" This is effectively the same obsession we have with finding our one true purpose; we just start our children off early.

I want my child to dream, to consider what the future may hold, to seek God's plan for His life above all else. I also don't want my son to *miss the trees for the forest* like I had for so many years. Just like you and me, our children have a Right Now Purpose. I'm not saying let's ditch all the future talk, but let's not forget to incorporate some present talk.

When Paul told Timothy to set an example for the believers, he started off with the statement, "Don't let anyone look down on you because you are young," 1 Timothy 4:12. Age is not a factor in being made a blessing. There are countless examples of young role models in the Bible: Miriam. Samuel. David. Mary. Jesus. Each person has a contribution. Some of the most precious prayers, sweetest encouragement, most thoughtful gifts, and most selfless acts of service have come from my son, Asa. He builds me up and inspires me too. Children are a blessing entrusted to us by God. It is never too early to begin teaching them that their one true purpose is to bring glory to God. That they can fulfill this purpose through their relationship with Him and their relationship with the people around them. Love God. Love others. And that the practical ways God allows us to show His love to others is by being a blessing. Every interaction is an opportunity to bless. Let's inspire our children to start asking what purpose God has for their lives today.

Engage

We can inspire others to bless by engaging them in our own blessing activities. Sometimes I approach blessing with a bit of self-focus—I only consider how I can be a blessing myself, and forget to bless others by inviting them to bless alongside me. To engage is to give others the opportunity to partner with us as a participant in the Blessing Cycle.

Every day people inspire others to bless by engaging them in acts of blessing.

When Mindy offered a sign-up to pray in 15-minute increments for a girl battling leukemia, she urged us to bless.

When Vivian provided our group with blank hand-crafted cards to encourage a hurting friend, she compelled us to bless.

When Maryann asked me to give Christmas gifts to a family she sponsored, she motivated me to bless.

When Sarah invited me to serve with her by cleaning the fire station where we meet for Life Group, she prompted me to bless.

When Cheryl challenged me to share a Bible verse on my timeline every day for a month, she stimulated me to bless.

Blessing begins in our homes. Our own people are in closest proximity to receive blessing from us and participate in blessing with us. It was especially easy for me to engage my child in blessing when he was younger because I set our schedule and dictated our daily activities.

I interrupted Asa's math lesson (he didn't mind at all) and asked him to pray with me. Mary had sent a message. "My dad has just been taken to the hospital. Please pray." In that moment, I invited Asa to partner in blessing Mary's family as we prayed together.

One of my favorite ways to inspire my son, to engage him in blessing, is to participate in Operation Christmas Child. Over the past few years, each November, Asa and I have set aside time for a special shopping trip with the sole purpose of buying gifts to pack in shoe boxes that are sent to needy children across the globe. He chooses items to pack a box for a boy; I fill a box for a girl. The time together is precious as we talk about the children who will receive our boxes, select just the right gifts, and strategically place each item to maximize the space. We are being a blessing; we are being blessed; we are building a tradition and making a memory.

Empower

When we set an example of blessing, express blessing, and engage others in our blessing activities, we cast a stone. When others respond by themselves being a blessing, a ripple is created by that stone. We can also actively create a ripple as we empower others to throw stones of their own. We launch others into blessing by providing tools, resources, and opportunities to bless. We propel others forward by helping them identify and put to use their own "such as I have" and bailiwick of blessing. As we inspire others to bless, they discover their Right Now Purpose. Empowerment is being a cheerleader: to encourage, support, and participate in someone else's blessing ventures.

In the last chapter, I introduced you to my mentor, Dianne. Not only did she come alongside me to build me up in my walk with Jesus, she continued by propelling me forward into my calling. I told you a little bit about the impact she has had on my writing. But even before that began, Dianne cheered me on and prayed me through starting the Bible study group I talked about at the end of *Share*. She also inspired me to bless by suggesting I sign up for our church's mentoring program again, this time as a mentor.

I was intimidated by the idea of mentoring because, of course, I felt unqualified. I was also concerned about who I may be paired with, but God knows what He's doing. I was matched with Trina, who sat across the room in the same Bible study, but we'd never actually met. We just so happened to only live a few miles apart and to have boys about the same age. In fact, we found we had a lot of things in common.

Mentoring another person in their relationship with Jesus was daunting, but as I discovered, it does not require me to be the perfect woman or a model Christian. Mentoring is about linking arms with a sister in Christ and moving forward in our walk together.

Trina's heart for the lost continues to inspire me. Before we were matched together, honestly, evangelism was not remotely on my radar. *Make Me a Blessing* was still a stirring in my heart; I was only in the very beginning stages of writing it. At that time, *Share* was not even a consideration for a bullet point, let alone an entire chapter. I was still of the mindset that someone else could catch them, and I'd grow them. Observing

Trina's sincere desire to see other people come to know Jesus and her passion for sharing the gospel makes me want to do the same.

I heard other mentors say it before, but it rang true in my own experience. I learned more from Trina and grew more from our relationship than I gave. That is how God works—it's the Blessing Cycle. We are blessed to be a blessing, and in the very act of blessing, we are often blessed in return.

Countless people have empowered me to pursue my calling, to use my gifts to be made a blessing. If I attempted to list them all, I would certainly miss someone important. But none of those people would desire recognition anyway. They selflessly blessed me without expectation.

To every person (you know who you are) who liked and shared my posts, watched my videos, read my devotions, previewed my work before I shared it with the rest of the world, supported me, encouraged me, prayed for me, promoted my writing, invited me to speak, shared your platform—Thank you! Thank you for propelling me forward in this journey. Your love has empowered me to be a blessing. I pray each one of you is blessed beyond measure, exceedingly abundantly above all you could ask or think.

CONCLUSION

You Have Arrived!

Driving isn't my favorite activity, especially while trying to navigate to an unfamiliar destination. I'm not great at following directions, and we live in the hills, where data connectivity is unreliable, to say the least. But I do manage to get around. One of the best parts of any trip is when I pull into a driveway or parking lot and my friend—the GPS lady—

cheers, "You have arrived." She actually says it with the same monotone voice that she says, "In a quarter mile, turn right onto Charlestown Road." But I like to imagine her clapping her hands while jumping up and down like there's a prize involved when she says, "You have arrived!" I usually answer her back. "Thank you for noticing!" I know I haven't arrived. I know I won't ever arrive this side of heaven. But for that one moment at the end of a journey, I enjoy imagining it just might be true.

"Not that I have already obtained all this, or have already arrived at my goal, but I press on to take hold of that for which Christ Jesus took hold of me," Philippians 3:12.

We won't ever arrive on our journey to be made a blessing. A lesson learned needs to continually be put into practice. Just when I thought I had this blessing thing down, I had what felt like a setback. Instead of pausing at the door to ask, "How am I going to bless someone where I'm going? What do I have to give?" I became focused on getting out the door, getting there on time, and what I looked like, everything else but blessing others. I had good intentions, but for well over a month, the book I meant to give sat on the bench next to the door. Why did I keep forgetting it? In fact, I couldn't remember blessing much at all in the past few weeks. Were the opportunities to bless getting sparse? No, of course not. There will never be a lack of need or a reduction in the call to bless. The truth is, I had stopped making blessing a priority. I let self-focus creep back in—one rushed morning, one tired afternoon, one busy evening at a time.

C.S. Lewis said, "We need to be continually reminded of what we believe. Neither this belief nor any other will automatically remain alive in the mind. It must be fed."[2] So true. Old, comfortable habits draw us in with elastic memory. If our heart's desire is ongoing effectiveness in being made a blessing, we must continue to count our blessings and acknowledge every good and perfect gift is from God Himself. We have to remember that we are blessed to bless and not to hoard. This means remaining vigilant to watch for the sickness of self that wants to sneak in and consume us. We must die daily, continue to beat down our flesh and never stop seeking MORE HE. less me. Keep pleading every day that we would be used in the Blessing Cycle; concede our plans and submit to His plans. Pray. Encourage. Give. Serve. Share. Inspire.

"We instructed you how to live in order to please God, as in fact you are living. Now we ask you and urge you in the Lord Jesus to do this more and more," 1 Thessalonians 4:1b.

Link arms with me one last time, let's encourage one another to keep up the good work! Don't grow weary in doing well! Continue to bring glory to God by being a blessing to others! Do this more and more!

Tessera

I lingered in the ancient art gallery taking in the intricate design of the piece entitled "Mosaic with Imago Clipeata of Bacchus." The photograph on the cover of this book is a detail from that very creation. A mosaic is a work of art, an image constructed as an artist strategically places tiny colored tiles called tesserae (tessera for singular). Nearly 10 feet in width and 10 feet in length, a work the size of the one I admired could be comprised of up to 80,000 individual tesserae. Can you imagine the tediousness of perfectly planning out and painstakingly placing every minute tile by hand? All the while, the artist keeps the big picture in mind.

"We are God's masterpiece," Ephesians 2:10a (NLT). Our Father is the Master Artist who understands the big picture is not formed by one glorious brush stroke. Like many of the mysteries of God, our human minds may never fully grasp the value of the small. Perspective is key in appreciating the captivating creation that is the mosaic of our lives. If we stand too close, the picture is indistinguishable; we only see what

198

looks like random, isolated, inconsequential tiles. When we try to zoom out so we can see the big picture, it doesn't seem to make sense. We no longer see the individual pieces that make up the work. An image appears to be forming, but we can't quite make out what it is.

"For now we see only a reflection as in a mirror; then we shall see face to face. Now I know in part; then I shall know fully, even as I am fully known," 1 Corinthians 13:12.

The mirrors used in ancient times were polished metal that did not produce a distinct image. In fact, the word used for reflection in this verse is where we get the word "enigma." We cannot fully comprehend the big picture because we only see a part, because it isn't finished. We are fully known by God, our past, present, and future. But He has yet to reveal the masterpiece of our lives because it is not complete; as long as we have breath, we are still a work of art in progress.

In the introduction, I cautioned that big picture thinking can keep us from seeing the trees while looking for the forest. Our Father meticulously places each minuscule blessing moment all the while keeping the big picture in mind. God, who knows the beginning from the end, simultaneously sees the forest and the trees. We, not so much. The vantage point makes all the difference. From a God's eye view, it all comes together, it all makes sense, but we can't see as He sees.

The big picture, the unique artwork of your life is not one big thing, it was never meant to be one big thing. Before He formed you, He planned your life to be a mosaic. Millions of nearly imperceptible, beautiful moments that create the masterpiece of your life. Each blessing is a tessera intricately planned out in advance by the Master Artist Himself.

"There has never been the slightest doubt in my mind that the God who started this great work in you would keep at it and bring it to a flourishing finish on the very day Christ Jesus appears," Philippians 1:6 (MSG).

You are a stunning masterpiece. The finished mosaic of your life promises to be breath-taking.

Final Blessing

The Lord spoke to Moses and instructed him to have Aaron bless the people of Israel with the words below from Numbers 6:24-26. Dear friend, before we part ways, please allow me the honor of speaking this blessing over you:

"The LORD bless you and keep you;
the LORD make his face shine on you and be gracious to you;
the LORD turn his face toward you and give you peace."

Father God, thank you for this dear sister who has joined me in learning to be made a blessing. I pray that You who began a good work in her would carry it on to completion until the day of Christ Jesus. Lord, that You would keep this message fresh in her heart. Reveal to my friend the good works You have planned in advance for her to do. Show her every day how to pray, encourage, give, serve, share, and inspire. Allow her to create an eternal ripple of blessing that extends far beyond her own circle of influence. Please continue the Blessing Cycle in Your child. Lord, bless her, and make her a blessing. In the holy name of Jesus, amen.

Acknowledgments

To my sweet Savior, Jesus. I cannot get over Your relentless pursuit of me. That You would see fit to use this broken jar of clay, well, that still blows my mind. Thank You! Without You I can do nothing.

To my dear husband, Chris. Thank you for traveling this crazy adventure with me. You recognized my gift before I ever understood it, and inspired me to embrace my calling as a communicator. You sacrificed time and resources and home-cooked meals to help me make this dream a reality. Before anyone else, you encouraged me to make it about the music. Your love and support mean everything. I love you.

To my best boy, Asa. I prayed every day for God to give you to us; I am eternally grateful He did. Loving you has given me the slightest glimpse of God's love for His children. Thank you for encouraging me to write, for being the first person to hear most of this book. You are wise beyond your years; your input made this project better. Even more so, in so many ways you set an example that taught me much of the content. You are kind and thoughtful and funny—no one makes me laugh like you do—that is a blessing!

I have labored over how to write the rest of these acknowledgments. There is such a desperate desire deep in my heart to not to leave anyone out, that I almost didn't name anyone. I could never possibly recount every person who has had an impact on my life. Family and friends and supporters.

Please know you are appreciated and valued and loved. Thank you. Every one of you.

There are a handful of people who were instrumental in the life of *Make Me a Blessing*. Without them, you would not be reading this today.

Dianne—mentoring me, encouraging me to write and speak and lead. That was more than I could have ever asked for. But that you agreed to link arms and walk alongside me every step of the way through this process, well, I don't have words. Your fingerprints are all over this book and all over my heart! Thank you for being faithful to Jesus and propelling me forward in my calling to serve Him.

My I2I friends (in alphabetical order)—Andrea, Brenda, Mary, Sheri—I cannot measure the impact you have had on my life and on this project, collectively and individually. Such grace upon grace that God would grow our hearts closer to Him and closer to each other.

Marti—thank you for believing in me and believing in this project. Your time and insights and direction helped propel me and the production of this book forward! I am beyond grateful for you and your leadership and your love!

Notes

Introduction Uniquely Unqualified

[1] 1 Samuel 17:45

[2] "Dead Poets Society." Buena Vista Pictures Distribution, 1989.

Chapter 1 The Heart of Blessing

[1] "The Most Influential People of All Time." *Ranker*, www.ranker.com/crowdranked-list/the-most-influential-people-of-all-time.

[2] Luke 18:5

[3] Wedge, Chris, and Carlos Saldanha. *Robots*. Blue Sky Studios, 20th Century Fox, 2005.

[4] James 2:16-17

[5] 1 Corinthians 13:1-3

Chapter 2 To Don't List

[1] Matthew 24:12, 2 Timothy 3:1-4

[2] C.S. Lewis, Mere Christianity (1952; Harper Collins 2001) 49.

[3] "Mary Poppins." Walt Disney Productions, 1964.

[4] 2 Corinthians 9:7

[5] Matthew 6:4

[6] Luke 6:34, Luke 14:14

[7] C.S. Lewis, Mere Christianity (1952; Harper Collins 2001) 56-57.

[8] Matthew 4:2

[9] Genesis 7:12

[10] Exodus 34:27-28

Chapter 3 Pray: Ask God to Meet Needs

[1] Note symbols chapter 3-7 indicate lyrics: Make Me A Blessing, [Hymn], Shuler, G. and Wilson, I., (1924).

[2] Psalm 10:12, 18

[3] Ham, Ken. "Bill Nye at Ark Encounter: Praying for Bill." *YouTube*, YouTube, 5 Aug. 2016, www.youtube.com/watch?v=4X5HWxOSDEc.

[4] Postal Service Mission and "Motto" – USPS, https://about.usps.com/who-we-are/postal-history/mission-motto.pdf

[5] Luke 11:1

[6] Luke 6:28b

[7] Colossians 4:3-4

Chapter 4 Encourage: Meet Emotional Needs

[1] Philippian 4:13

[2] 2 Corinthians 12:9
[3] James 1:19
[4] "Bambi." Walt Disney, 1942.
[5] Markus, Christopher, et al. *Chronicles of Narnia, the Voyage of the Dawn Treader*. 20th Century Fox, 2010.

Chapter 5 Give: Meet Material Needs

[1] C.S. Lewis, Mere Christianity (1952; Harper Collins 2001) 86.
[2] Henry H. Halley, Halley's Bible Handbook (1927; Zondervan 1962) 352.
[3] Acts 20:35b

Chapter 6 Serve: Meet Physical Needs

[1] "A Quote by Martin Luther King Jr." *Goodreads*, Goodreads, www.goodreads.com/quotes/757.
[2] James 1:6,8
[3] "Ronald Reagan Quotes." *BrainyQuote*, Xplore, www.brainyquote.com/quotes/ronald_reagan_120491.
[4] 1 Timothy 4:14
[5] 2 Timothy 1:6
[6] 2 Timothy 1:7 (ESV)
[7] "Mother Teresa: 'Do Small Things with Great Love'." *America Magazine*, 1 Sept. 2017, www.americamagazine.org/faith/2016/08/09/mother-teresa-do-small-things-great-love.

Chapter 7 Share: Meet Spiritual Needs

[1] K. P. Yohannan, No Longer a Slumdog: Bringing Hope to Children in Crisis (GFA Books 2012).
[2] Exodus 4:1b
[3] The Brady Bunch, Johnston, William. "The Driver's Seat." Season 5, episode 15, 1974.
[4] Revelation 21:8
[5] Matthew 25:46
[6] 2 Thessalonians 1:9
[7] Matthew 13:50
[8] Mark 9:43
[9] Romans 2:4b (NASB)
[10] John 4:39a
[11] John 4:41

Chapter 8 Inspire: Compel Others to Meet Needs

[1] "A Quote by Mother Teresa." *Goodreads*, Goodreads, www.goodreads.com/quotes/49502
[2] C.S. Lewis, Mere Christianity (1952; Harper Collins 2001) 141.

About the Author

Cassia Elder is an author, speaker, and women's ministry leader. It is her joy to connect with an online audience through her website and social media where she has conversations about real life, engages with Scripture, and navigates the practical application of how those two things fit together. What fills her cup most is to have these authentic conversations with women in person—to hug their necks, hear their stories, and share the truth of God's Word.

Cassia lives in Southern Indiana on a nearly-off-grid microfarm with her husband Chris, their son Asa, and a porch-sittin' hound dog named Moonshine. Their days are spent restoring a rustic log cabin on the creek and exploring nature. Most mornings you'll find Cassia rocking in her Grandma Phyllis's hand-me-down glider on the back porch with a mug of coffee in her hand and a Bible in her lap. She is a nerd for God's Word who enjoys gardening and has been passionate about crafting with words since joining the Young Author's Club in the fourth grade.

Connect
with Cassia

🏀 CassiaElder.com

f Cassia Elder-Author

📷 @cassiaelder

🐦 @eldercassia

Tweetable and Repeatable

SOME OF OUR FAVORITE QUOTES FROM
Make Me a Blessing

➢ Your purpose is not tied up in your 5-year plan. You have a Right Now Purpose.
➢ Gratitude is the catalyst to being made a blessing.
➢ The heart of blessing is having a heart to bless.
➢ Self-focus is the #1 enemy of blessing.
➢ MORE HE. less me.
➢ Prayer is not passive; it is warfare.
➢ Be a searchin' and speakin' positive pointer-outer.
➢ Let your story bring God glory.
➢ God wants our firstfruits not our leftovers.
➢ Our best witness is our walk.

Spread the Word

• FREE *Make Me a Blessing* resources at CassiaElder.com
• Share the book on social media with the hashtag #MakeMeABlessingBook
  ▪ On Facebook tag Cassia Elder- Author
  ▪ On Twitter tag @eldercassia
  ▪ On Instagram tag @cassiaelder
• Write a book review on Amazon and GoodReads

www.ingramcontent.com/pod-product-compliance
Lightning Source LLC
Chambersburg PA
CBHW051725040426
42447CB00008B/972